Tackle Bridge

Tackle Bridge

E. P. C. COTTER

STANLEY PAUL, LONDON

STANLEY PAUL & CO LTD
3 Fitzroy Square, London W1

An imprint of the Hutchinson Publishing Group

London Melbourne Sydney Auckland
Wellington Johannesburg Cape Town
and agencies throughout the world

First published 1962
Revised edition October 1973
Second impression July 1975
© E. P. C. Cotter 1962

Printed in Great Britain by litho by The Anchor Press Ltd
and bound by Wm Brendon & Son Ltd
both of Tiptree, Essex

ISBN 0 09 118160 7 (cased)
0 09 118161 5 (paper)

To my brother
TERENCE
who really is a good partner

My grateful thanks to Victor Berger
for kind assistance in reading the
proofs and for helpful suggestions.

Contents

Illustrations

Foreword

For many years now 'Pat' Cotter has been one of the leading Bridge players in this country. He has been a very successful rubber Bridge player as well as a Gold Cup winner and a British representative in the European Championship.

His middle name is versatility and, apart from his Bridge career, he has long been a leading Croquet player and a former scratch golfer. Since he has also been Senior Classics master at St. Paul's School, it must be child's play to him to teach Bridge.

He has brought to this book the talent of an expert in introducing beginners to the 'Kingdom of cards'. Therein live fifty-two characters and he is friendly with them all.

His object is not to just teach the game but to pass on to his readers some of the obvious enjoyment which he has himself obtained from knowing His Majesty, the King of Spades, and some of the skill he has on occasion displayed in forcing such lowly characters as the Two of Diamonds and the Two of Clubs to play a major part in the game.

As a book for beginners, I find *Tackle Bridge* quite excellent. I am sure that it will give pleasure to many and I wish the author all the success which he so richly deserves.

K. W. KONSTAM

Introduction

In my introduction to *Tackle Croquet This Way* I said that I was faced by a problem which would not arise if I were writing on Contract Bridge, because I had to explain not only how to play Croquet but what Croquet was. I was quite sure that writing on Bridge for this series would be far easier. How wrong I was! The Croquet book unfolded itself easily and naturally, but when I came to write this book, though the way seemed clear up to a point, it was darkened by the problem of what to leave out.

Bridge is a game of infinite variety—hence its charm. One could easily write on the play alone a book comparable in size to *War and Peace*. So to cater for the complete beginner within the limits of this book meant inevitably that much that I would like to include would have to be sacrificed.

It was clear that it was the play that must be sacrificed to the bidding. A beginner can more readily assimilate instruction on the bidding, for it may be explained clearly and briefly. The play of the cards, however, even in its simpler variations, needs essentially to be practised. A player can never grasp how to play a four-card trump suit either from a book or from verbal instruction. It is the practical experience, gleaned from mistakes in actual play, that is the real teacher.

For all that, I have tried to deal with the basic principles underlying No Trumps and suit play. From this the reader will, I hope, grasp the logic behind the play of the cards.

If the bidding methods suggested are understood and put into practice, I am sure that the reader will be a sound bidder and trusted by his partners, good and indifferent alike.

Yes, be a good partner, courteous, kind and sympathetic. That is worth more than mere technique.

E.P.C.C.

Preliminaries

The Game
Contract Bridge is a game played with one pack of playing cards.

Players
Bridge is a game for four players; two, sitting opposite each other, constituting a side against the other two. Thus 'North' and 'South' play against 'East' and 'West'.

Equipment
A table, four chairs, two packs of cards, four scoring pads and pencils.

Pack of Cards
A pack of cards consists of fifty-two cards divided into four suits, each of thirteen cards.

The Suits
The suits and their symbols are:

Spades (♠), Hearts (♡), Diamonds (♢), Clubs (♣).

Spades and Hearts are called Major suits, Diamonds and Clubs are called Minor suits.

Rank of Suits
The suits rank (for bidding purposes) in the above order, Spades being the highest, Clubs the lowest.

The Cards
Each suit consists of thirteen cards that rank in the following order:

Ace (highest), King, Queen, Knave, Ten, Nine, Eight, Seven, Six, Five, Four, Three, Two.

The five highest cards, Ace (A), King (K), Queen (Q), Knave (J) and Ten, are called Honour Cards. The Knave is also called the Jack, hence the abbreviation J.

Drawing for Partners

One pack of cards is spread out face downwards on the table. Each player draws one card. When all four have drawn, the four cards are turned face upwards. The two highest play against the two lowest. If the four cards drawn are the Seven of Diamonds, the King of Clubs, the Three of Clubs and the Ten of Spades, the King and Ten play against the Seven and Three.

If two or more cards of the same rank are drawn, the rank of the suits determines the precedence. If the four cards drawn are the Ace of Spades, the King of Hearts, the King of Diamonds and the Two of Clubs, the Ace of Spades and the King of Hearts play against the King of Diamonds and the Two of Clubs.

Drawing the Highest Card

The highest card drawn confers upon the player drawing it three privileges:
1. The first deal.
2. The choice of cards. He may choose which pack (say Red or Blue) he wishes to deal.
3. The choice of seats. He may choose which of the four seats he wishes to occupy. When he has chosen, his partner must sit opposite, one opponent must sit on his right, the other on his left.

The Shuffle

The player on the dealer's left takes the cards chosen by the dealer, shuffles them and places them face downwards on his right. The dealer then picks them up, may shuffle them himself if he wishes, and places them on his right for his right-hand opponent to cut.

The Cut

The right-hand opponent divides the pack into two portions, lifting off the top of the pack not fewer than four nor more than forty-eight cards, and placing this portion beside the lower portion on the table.

Completing the Cut

The dealer completes the cut by placing the lower portion on top of the upper portion. The dealer is now ready to deal.

The Deal

The dealer distributes the cards face downwards, one at a time, to each player, starting with the left-hand opponent and proceeding in a clockwise direction until all fifty-two cards are dealt.

Picking up the Dealt Cards

When all the cards have been dealt and NOT BEFORE each player picks up the thirteen cards in front of him. These constitute his 'hand'.

The Second Pack and Rotation of Deal

While the dealer is dealing the Blue pack, his partner should shuffle the Red pack and place it face downwards on his right ready for the next deal.

The deal passes in turn to the player on the left of the previous dealer. Thus if South deals the first hand, West deals the second, North the third and so on.

Sorting the Hand

To enable a player to see clearly what he has been dealt, he should sort his hand into suits and arrange each suit in ranking order. It is also helpful to alternate red and black suits.

The four players, each holding thirteen cards, are now ready to play a game of Bridge. What they do will be discussed in the next chapter.

Quiz on Chapter 1

1. Which are the Major suits?
2. Who shuffles the pack for the dealer?
3. In what order do the suits rank?
4. In drawing for partners the Four of Hearts, the Two of Spades the Three of Clubs and the Three of Diamonds are drawn. Who plays with the Three of Diamonds?
5. What three privileges does drawing the highest card confer?

2

The Auction and the Play

EACH hand is divided into two parts, the Auction, which is a tender for Contract, and the Play, which is fulfilment of Contract.

As it is the Auction that decides which player is to be Declarer and play the hand, it must take place before the Play begins. Now the Bridge player, though he is ultimately bidding for *points*, is at the beginning more like a contracting engineer making a tender for a project such as a highway fly-over. He must have the necessary qualifications and financial backing before he can even think of making a tender. There is a rival firm, represented by his opponents, in the market, and if their assets are greater than his then they are going to secure the contract.

The Bridge player does not bid for points, but he offers to deliver (win) a certain number of Tricks. The Contract goes to the side making the highest bid. If this side is able to fulfil its obligations its Tricks become realizable assets in the shape of points. But if the side is unable to make good its promise there is legal machinery to penalize it for its defaulting.

Before we go any further into the question of bidding, there are a few technical terms that must be explained.

Tricks

There are four cards in a Trick, each player contributing one. It is clear that there are thirteen Tricks in every hand or deal.

The Book

The first six Tricks that the declarer wins constitute the Book, and they do not count towards his score. When a player bids One in any denomination he is in reality contracting to win the odd Trick over the Book, or seven Tricks in all. Similarly, if he bids Seven he is contracting to win all thirteen Tricks.

Trumps and No Trumps

When a player makes a bid he must either name one of the four suits as trumps or specify another denomination known as No Trumps.

The word 'trump' is connected with the word 'triumph' and the trump suit can triumph over the other suits, so that the lowly Two of the trump suit can capture the lordly Ace of another suit. This precedence of the trump suit is subject to the rule of 'following suit', which you will learn about later.

If a player specifies No Trumps it means that he does not want to have any suit as trumps.

You have learnt about the order in which the suits rank for bidding purposes, *but No Trumps outranks any suit.*

The Bid or Call

A bid is a tender for a specified number of Tricks.

A call is any bid, No bid, Double or Re-double.

Each player in turn, starting with the dealer, is entitled to make at least one bid or call. No player is obliged to make a positive tender—he can always say No Bid.

If all four players say No Bid, there is no tender and so no fulfilment of Contract. The deal is at once abandoned, and the next player in rotation deals with the other pack.

The dealer may call No Bid, or name any number from One to Seven in No Trumps or in a suit.

The next player, and each player in turn thereafter, may call No Bid, or name any number in No Trumps or in a suit, provided that his bid names either a greater number of Tricks than the last bid or an equal number in a denomination of higher rank.

Double and Re-double

There are two other calls which can occur during the Auction. Any player may, in his turn, double the last bid if it was made by an opponent. As a Double increases the premiums and penalties for the Declarer, according to the success or failure of his contract, it does, in effect, challenge the Declarer's ability to meet his liabilities.

Any player may, in his turn, re-double the last bid if it was made by his own side and has been doubled by an opponent.

Termination of the Auction

The Auction terminates when any bid, Double or Re-double is followed by three consecutive calls of No Bid.

Let us take an imaginary Auction as follows:

South deals and bids One Spade, West says Two Clubs, North says No Bid, East bids Two Diamonds. On the second round of bidding South says Three Spades, West says No Bid, North bids Four Spades, East says No Bid. On the third round South says No Bid and West says No Bid. That ends the Auction as there have been three consecutive No Bids or passes.

Let us examine the bidding in detail. South, by bidding One Spade, undertakes to win for his side Seven Tricks with Spades as trumps. West says Two Clubs—he cannot say One Club because Clubs rank below Spades—thereby promising to win eight Tricks. North passes, and East suggests an alternative eight-Trick Contract in Diamonds. It is sufficient for him to call Two Diamonds because Diamonds outrank Clubs. South now calls Three Spades. Two Spades would have been enough but South wants to show a good hand, by offering to make nine Tricks. West passes, but North, though he has previously said No Bid, feels justified in bidding for ten Tricks, which as you will learn later is enough for Game.

It will be good for you to see the above bidding sequence written out in Bridge abbreviation.

S	W	N	E
1 ♠	2 ♣	No	2 ◇
3 ♠	No	4 ♠	No
No	No	—	—

What has emerged from this Auction? Two things have been determined:

The Contract

The Contract (*or* Final Contract) is the highest bid of the Auction, and the side making the final bid becomes the Declaring Side.

The Declarer is that member of the Declaring Side who *first* named the denomination of the Contract.

If we refer to the bidding table above we shall see that the highest bid was made by North, so that the Contract is Four Spades. North and South therefore become the Declaring Side. The Declarer, however, is South, because he was the first to name the denomination Spades.

This brings us to the point where the Play begins.

The Defending Side

The opponents of the Declarer are known as the Defending Side or the Defenders.

Lead to the First Trick

The Declarer's left-hand opponent makes the first lead. He may lead any card that he chooses.

Dummy

As soon as the opening lead has been made the Declarer's partner lays his cards face upwards on the table in front of him. He is known as Dummy, and takes no active part in the Play. The Declarer plays both his own hand and the Dummy.

Play to a Trick

After a card has been led by the Leader to a Trick each of the other three players, in strict clockwise rotation, must play a card to complete the Trick. He must 'follow suit' if able to do so; that is, he must play a card of the same suit as the Lead. If he has no card of the suit led he is free to play any card that he may hold.

Winning of Tricks

Each Trick is won by the highest card *of the suit led*, unless there is a trump suit, when it is won by the highest trump.

Lead to subsequent Tricks

To all Tricks subsequent to the first Trick the lead is made by the winner of the previous Trick.

Termination of Play

Play continues until all thirteen Tricks have been completed.

Let us now play through an imaginary hand and see the mechanics of Leads and Tricks. Here is the hand set out in the usual diagrammatic form:

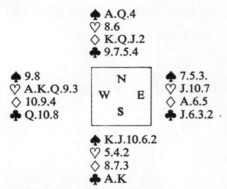

```
                    ♠ A.Q.4
                    ♡ 8.6
                    ◇ K.Q.J.2
                    ♣ 9.7.5.4
    ♠ 9.8                          ♠ 7.5.3.
    ♡ A.K.Q.9.3     ┌─────────┐    ♡ J.10.7
    ◇ 10.9.4        │    N    │    ◇ A.6.5
    ♣ Q.10.8        │ W     E │    ♣ J.6.3.2
                    │    S    │
                    └─────────┘
                    ♠ K.J.10.6.2
                    ♡ 5.4.2
                    ◇ 8.7.3
                    ♣ A.K
```

The Contract is Four Spades. The Declarer is South.

Trick 1

West leads because he is the left-hand opponent. He leads the Ace of Hearts (♡ A) and North faces his cards.

South, playing both hands, plays the Six of Hearts from dummy (♡ 6)

East plays the Seven of Hearts (♡ 7)

South plays from his own hand the Two of Hearts (♡ 2).

Notice that North, East and South hold Hearts in their hands so they are obliged to play them.

A player must play a card of the same suit as the Lead if able to do so.

The Trick is won by West with the Ace—one Trick to the Defenders.

Trick 2

West leads because he is the winner of the previous Trick.

He leads ♡ K, and North, East and South follow with ♡ 8 ♡ 10 and ♡ 4.

West wins the Trick with the King—two Tricks to the Defenders.

Trick 3

West, still the leader, leads ♡ Q.

North, having no more Hearts, is free to play any card. He plays ♠ 4.

East and South follow with ♡ J and ♡ 5.

North wins the Trick with ♠ 4, because he has played a trump which 'takes' a card of any other suit—one Trick to the Declarer.

Trick 4

North leads ♠ A, and East, South and West follow with ♠ 3, ♠ 2, ♠ 8.

North wins—two Tricks to the Declarer.

Trick 5

North leads ♠ Q. East, South and West follow with ♠ 5, ♠ 6, ♠ 9.
North wins—three Tricks to the Declarer.

Trick 6

North leads ♣ 4, East plays ♣ 2, South plays ♣ K, West plays ♣ 8.
South wins—four Tricks to the Declarer.

Trick 7

South leads ♠ K, West plays ♡ 3, North plays ♣ 5, East plays ♠ 7.

Neither West nor North are able to follow, but as it is the trump suit that has been led the cards that they discard cannot affect the winning of the Trick.

South wins—five Tricks to the Declarer.

Trick 8

South leads ♢ 3, West plays ♢ 4, North plays ♢ J, East plays ♢ A.
East wins—three Tricks to the Defenders.

Trick 9

East leads ♣ 3, South plays ♣ A, West plays ♣ 10, North plays ♣ 7.

South wins—six Tricks to the Declarer.

Trick 10

South leads ♢ 7, West plays ♢ 9, North plays ♢ Q, East plays ♢ 5.
North wins—seven Tricks to the Declarer.

Trick 11

North leads ♢ K, and the other players follow.
North wins—eight Tricks to the Declarer.

Trick 12 and 13

These Tricks must be won by South as he has the only two trumps left—ten Tricks to the Declarer.

The result of the hand is that the Declaring Side have won ten Tricks and the Defending Side have won three Tricks. North and South have made their Contract and score 120 below the line (see next chapter).

Quiz on Chapter 2

1. When does the Auction end?
2. Who becomes the Declarer?
3. If all four players say No Bid what happens?
4. What is the Book?
5. In a No Trump Contract West leads ♣ 9, North plays ♢ Q, East plays ♡ K, and South plays ♠ A. Who wins the Trick?

Contract Bridge Scoring Table

TRICK POINTS

Suit Bids	♠	♡	♢	♣	No Trumps Bids	
					First Trick	Subsequent Tricks
Each Trick bid and made	30	30	20	20	40	30
if doubled	60	60	40	40	80	60
if re-doubled	120	120	80	80	160	120

Game is 100 Points, made up of Trick Points

PREMIUM POINTS

Undertricks	Not Vulnerable	Vulnerable
Each Undertrick Counts	50	100
If doubled		
First Undertrick counts	100	200
Subsequent Undertricks count	200	300
If redoubled		
First Undertrick counts	200	400
Subsequent Undertricks count	400	600

A side that has scored one Game is said to be *vulnerable*

BONUS POINTS

	Not Vulnerable	Vulnerable
1. Overtricks		
Each Trick made over Contract	Trick value	Trick value
if doubled	100	200
if re-doubled	200	400
2. Fulfilment of doubled or re-doubled		
Contract	50	50
3. Slams		
Small Slam bid and made	500	750
Grand Slam bid and made	1000	1500
4. Rubber		
If opponents win no Game	700	
If opponents win one Game	500	
For one Game in unfinished Rubber	300	
For part-score in unfinished Game	50	

HONOUR POINTS

For holding Four Honours of the Trump Suit in one Hand	100
For holding Five Honours of the Trump Suit in one Hand	150
For holding Four Aces at No Trumps in one Hand	150

3

The Object of the Game

AT CRICKET the object of the batting side is to score runs, the object of the fielding side is to allow as few runs as possible to be scored against them. It is much the same at Contract Bridge. The object of the Declaring Side is to score Points, the object of the Defending Side is to allow as few Points as possible to be scored against them. There is, however, one great difference—the fielding side at Cricket can never score runs, but the Defending Side at Bridge can score Points.

Having established that the object of Bridge is to score Points, let us see what these Points are and how they are scored. If you study the Table on the preceding pages in the light of explanations that follow, you should be able to grasp the whole principle on which the scoring is based.

Trick Points

These are won *only* by the Declaring Side, and *only* when the Contract is fulfilled.

These Points and no others score below the line, that is, count towards the Game.

Premium Points

These are divided into three classes—Penalty, Bonus and Honour. Penalty Points are won only by the Defending Side, and only when the Contract is defeated.

Bonus points are won only by the Declaring Side through:

1. Overtricks.
2. Fulfilment of doubled or re-doubled Contract.
3. Slams.
4. The Rubber.

Honour Points

These are scored usually by the Declaring Side, more rarely by the Defending Side. They are the result neither of good bidding nor of good play. They depend upon the fortuitous distribution of the cards in the Deal. They have been given up mostly in Duplicate Tournaments, and their excision from Rubber Bridge is overdue.

Let us now clarify the situation by examples. Under TRICK POINTS you see that GAME is made up of 100 Trick Points. These can be won by bidding and making

1. Three No Trumps $40 + 30 + 30 = 100$
2. Four Spades or Hearts $4 \times 30 = 120$
3. Five Diamonds or Clubs $5 \times 20 = 100$
4. Two spades Doubled $2 \times 60 = 120$
5. One No Trumps Re-doubled $1 \times 160 = 160$.
And so on.

Remember that what you write down below the line when you fulfil your Contract is the number of Tricks mentioned in your bid multiplied by the Trick value. For example, you bid three Spades and make four. You write 90 below the line (3×30) and 30 above (one overtrick). Again you bid one Club, it is doubled and re-doubled, and you make eight Tricks. You write 80 below the line (1×80) and 200 above (or 400 if vulnerable) for one overtrick.

You do not have to score these 100 Points in one Contract. You can have two or more bites at the cherry, provided that the opponents do not score 100 first, for a side making Game deprives its opponents of any part-score that they may have. For example, you have 60 below the line and your opponents have 40, in the first game. If you bid and make two Clubs this 40 Points gives you Game, and the second game is started at Love all. Your opponents can no longer use their 40 Points towards Game, though they get the credit for it in the final addition.

Under PREMIUM POINTS you will see that a side that has scored Game is said to be vulnerable. Conversely, a side that has not scored Game is said to be non-vulnerable. These clumsy terms still persist, because no one has thought of anything better. When you are vulnerable the penalties and some of the rewards are increased —that is all there is to it.

Now let us take an imaginary Rubber lasting six hands, and see how to record it on the scoring pad. Suppose that you and I cut together and that you deal the first hand. We secure the Contract with a bid of Three Hearts—you play the hand and make eleven Tricks. You and I write on our scoring pads 90 below and 60 above thus. Note that the black line across the middle divides Trick Points from Premium Points. The first scores should be near the line, the Trick Points working downwards, the Premium Points upwards.

60	
90	

On the second hand our opponents bid one No Trumps and make one Over-trick.

Now we enter the score that 'they' have made, and this is how our score pads should read now. Both sides have a part-score towards the Game.

60	30
90	40

On the third hand there is a struggle for the Contract. Our opponents bid up to Three Hearts but we outbid them with Three Spades and we have no difficulty in making ten Tricks. I played the hand and as I held Ace, Queen, Knave and Ten of trumps in my own hand I get 100 Honour Points. The score now reads:

100	
30	
60	30
90	
90	40

We draw a line under this as we have made Game and our opponents lose their part-score.

We are now vulnerable and the fourth hand is dealt. Our opponents bid Four Hearts but we decide to bid Four Spades to save the Game. We are doubled and only make eight Tricks. This means that our opponents score 500 Penalty Points. So we enter this and here is the present position:

100	
30	500
60	30
90	
90	40

The fifth hand is played by the opponents in a Contract of Three Diamonds which they just make. This gives them another part-score which counts towards this second Game. Here is the score:

100	
30	500
60	30
90	
90	40
	60

In the sixth and last hand we bid Four Hearts. Our left-hand opponent doubles but we manage to make ten Tricks. At this stage we have not only to enter the score for the current hand, but also to add up and see what the result of the Rubber is. After we have written 240 below and 50 above for Fulfilment of Doubled Contract and 700 for Rubber where opponents have won no Game, we add up both sides and subtract the opposing score from our own. The answer is 730. That means that we have won 700 Points.

700	
50	
100	
30	500
60	30
90	
90	40
240	60
1360	630
630	
730	

Quiz on Chapter 3

1. Where are Trick Points scored and by whom?

2. What is the Bonus for bidding and making a Small Slam when not vulnerable?

3. You bid Four No Trumps and make Six. How is it scored?

4. What is the Bonus for making a Contract (a) when doubled, (b) when re-doubled?

5. What Points can the Defenders score?

4

The Purpose of Bidding.
Hand Valuation

THE purpose of bidding is to enable a partnership to reach a Contract which will gain them the maximum or *lose them the minimum* number of Points.

At every session of Bridge the hands fall into two categories, uncontested and competitive. In uncontested hands one side or the other has the preponderance of the high cards or the distribution, and is left to bid with little or no interference from the opponents. The disparity between the two sides is too great to admit of any opposition. In competitive hands, however, either both sides have good suits, or the distribution of one side is able to offset the high cards of the other. A spirited Auction ensues, with each side seeking to push its opponents to the breaking-point.

In uncontested hands the partners bid up to whatever Contract they think they are capable of fulfilling. By exchange of information they seek to find out two things—Place and Height. Place is *where* to play, whether in No Trumps, Spades, Hearts, Diamonds or Clubs. Height is *how much* to play, whether part-score, Game or Slam. Here good bidding reaches a Contract that gains the maximum number of Points for the partnership.

In competitive hands, on the contrary, we are faced with a new factor—Opponents' Potential. One side or the other may be prepared to make a 'sacrifice' bid, that is to force its opponents to accept Penalty Points instead of Trick Points. This phase of bidding will be dealt with in the chapter on Defensive Bidding. You will remember that it was hinted at on page 25, where 'we' decided to bid Four Spades to save the Four Hearts that 'they' had bid.

It is clear that in both cases some method of hand valuation is essential, in order that partners may assess the Trick-taking capacity of their cards. This will check excessive ambition in uncontested hands and avoid incurring a loss on good cards. Again it will prevent them from paying too high a price in Penalty Points when attempting to outbid the opponents, or to accept too low a price when the opponents try a sacrifice.

One thing must be appreciated at the outset. The thirteen cards that constitute a Bridge hand have two values, a defensive value and an attacking value. In defence, that is when the opponents have secured the Contract, we can count on taking Tricks only with our first- and second-round winners, with Aces and Kings. In attack, however, we can promote the low cards of our long suits into eventual winners. For example, if you hold the following hand:

♠ A.K.Q.J.10.7.6.3
♡ 7.4
◇ 6
♣ 9.5

it is clear that you will be able to take eight tricks at your own Spade declaration. This is a very easy hand to assess. The solid Spade suit guarantees eight Tricks—these we call Playing Tricks. It should be equally clear to you that you cannot take more than two Tricks against an opposing Contract in one of the other three suits, and you will most likely take one or none.

In most cases when you open the bidding you cannot be sure whether your side or the opponents are going to play the hand. Therefore your opening bid must generally indicate not only Playing Tricks but Defensive Tricks. Without this defensive guarantee your side would never be able to tell when the opponents had bid for a number of Tricks they were unable to fulfil.

Let us consider another hand from a different angle:

	Defensive Tricks	Point Count	Playing Tricks
♠ A.K.9.6.3	2	7	4
♡ A.J.10	1	5	1
◇ K.Q	1	5	1
♣ Q.J.10	0	3	1
	—	—	—
	4	20	7
	—	—	—

The first two columns are easily understood, but the third one needs a little explanation. When we value the hand with Spades as trumps we count 2 for the Ace and King, and 2 for the long cards. Until we learn something of the distribution from the bidding we assume that the unseen Spades are divided 3—3—2 and give the Queen to the opponents. Thus after the opponents have taken their Queen the two small cards become good, and we take four Tricks in the suit. Though we count only one Trick for the Hearts we do not ignore the Plus Value of the J and 10.

The dual value of a hand from the offensive and defensive standpoints has given birth to various methods of hand valuation from Honour Trick to Point Count. But neither system is *by itself* able to assess accurately the Trick-taking capacity of a hand.

Let us consider this hand:

♠ A.K.2
♡ A.K.2
◇ A.K.2
♣ A.K.3.2

The Honour Trick Table assesses this at 8 Honour Tricks. Now 8 H.T. are supposed to develop 5 low card Tricks, but even the veriest neophyte knows that thirteen Tricks cannot be taken without fair assistance from partner. The Milton Work Point Count, which counts an Ace = 4, a King = 3, a Queen = 2, and a Knave = 1, values this hand at 28 Points. Now let us turn to the following hand:

♠ A.K.5.4.3.2
♡ A.K.5.4.3.2
◇ 2
♣ —

This hand possesses half the number of Honour Tricks and half the number of Points. The H.T. table tells us that we can expect to take seven Tricks, while the Point Count tells us that with 14 Points we have little over a minimum. Yet reason tells us that we need from partner little more than three or four cards in one of our suits to take ten Tricks and reason is confirmed by Playing Tricks which amount to 10.

The Point Count has to a large extent superseded the H.T. method but it is quite impossible to assess your points accurately unless some adjustment is made for distribution. I have for many years employed the Point Count for No Trumps bidding, as it is most accurate on the balanced hands, where no distributional adjustment is necessary. But for purposes of suit bidding no player can expect to get far if he is a slave to Points. However, we will leave the discussion of the distributional valuation of a hand until we deal with the question of suit bidding. We will start the next chapter by considering No Trumps bidding.

Quiz on Chapter 4
1. What is the Milton Work Point Count?
2. What is the purpose of a sacrifice bid?

3. How many Points has this hand:

    ♠ A.Q.7.4   ♡ K.J.8.6   ◇ A.J.10   ♣ K.Q

4. What are Place and Height in bidding?
5. What is a Defensive Trick?

5

No Trumps Bidding

IT IS logical to start with No Trumps bidding, because, as I said before, the Point Count is an accurate method of valuation, as no distributional adjustment is necessary, and there are no ruffling tricks to complicate the issue. Let us look once again at the Point Count table:

$$Ace = 4, \quad King = 3, \quad Queen = 2, \quad Knave = 1$$

The Opening Bid of One No Trump

To qualify for an opening bid of One No Trumps your hand must satisfy three requirements—Points, Pattern and Protection.

1. Points. Not fewer than 16 and not more than 18.
2. Pattern. Either 4—3—3—3, 4—4—3—2, or more rarely 5—3—3—2.
3. Protection. At least three suits stopped. The beginner will do well to aim at having all four suits stopped. Whatever happens see that your unguarded suit is of at least three cards. To bid No Trumps with a losing doubleton is not to be recommended.

Sure stoppers are:

> Ace
> K.Q
> Q.J.10
> J.10.9.8

We cannot always enjoy the luxury of sure stoppers in every suit, and a little latitude is allowed. The following are accepted as stoppers:

K.2
Q.10.2
J.4.3.2

To hold Q.10.2 in a suit is not regarded as a very sure Protection and with only Q.3.2 you should look for a different opening bid.

Here are some examples of correct No Trumps bids:

1.	♠ K.J.7.2	2. ♠ A.10.8	3. ♠ A.8.7
	♡ A.9.7	♡ A.7	♡ Q.10.6
	◇ A.Q.8	◇ A.9.4.2	◇ K.9
	♣ K.10.3	♣ A.8.6.4	♣ A.K.Q.6.3

The first hand is 4—3—3—3 and has 17 Points.

The second hand is 4—4—3—2 and has 16 Points.

The third hand is 5—3—3—2 and has a maximum Point Count of 18. Each of these hands could be opened with a bid of one in a suit, but it is well to open one No Trumps when you have the qualifications. Once you limit your hand either upwards or downwards you make subsequent bidding easier. If your partner knows the limit of your hand he is able to tell you by his response what the expectations of the partnership are. This will be dealt with more fully when the responses to No Trumps bids are considered.

The Opening Bid of Two No Trumps

Of the three requirements needed for the One No Trumps bid Pattern remains unchanged, but Points and Protection have to be adjusted as follows:

Points. The range is narrow—21 or 22.
Protection. All four suits must be stopped.

You will see that balanced hands with 19 or 20 Points are not included in either category. They are too strong for One No Trumps and not strong enough for Two No Trumps. These must be opened with a suit bid of one.

The Opening Bid of Three No Trumps

For this bid Pattern and Protection remain the same as for Two No Trumps, but Points must fall between 25 and 27.

Here again you see that there is an intermediate zone, and that hands counting 23 or 24 have to be specially treated. By far the best method, adopted by most players today, is to open balanced hands of 23 or 24 Points with a conventional Two Club bid (see chapter 13) and to rebid Two No Trumps if partner responds with a negative bid of Two Diamonds. The whole question of bidding balanced hands with a count of more than 22 is dealt with on page 71.

Quiz on Chapter 5
Of the following hands:

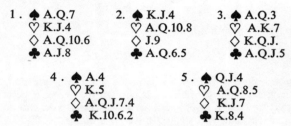

1 . ♠ A.Q.7   2. ♠ K.J.4   3 . ♠ A.Q.3
    ♡ K.J.4   ♡ A.Q.10.8   ♡ A.K.7
    ◇ A.Q.10.6   ◇ J.9   ◇ K.Q.J.
    ♣ A.J.8   ♣ A.Q.6.5   ♣ A.Q.J.5

    4 . ♠ A.4   5 . ♠ Q.J.4
        ♡ K.5   ♡ A.Q.8.5
        ◇ A.Q.J.7.4   ◇ K.J.7
        ♣ K.10.6.2   ♣ K.8.4

Three may be opened with a bid of No Trumps.
Which are they and what should each bid be?
Two may not be opened with a bid of No Trumps.
Which are they and why do they not qualify?

6

No Trumps Responses to an Opening No Trumps

NOTHING is easier than responding to the No Trumps bid, for it is a question of simple arithmetic. A pack of cards contains 40 Points. When a partnership contracts for nine Tricks by bidding 3 NT it undertakes to win slightly more than $\frac{5}{8}$ of the Tricks. To fulfil this undertaking it requires slightly more than $\frac{5}{8}$ of the Points. This gives us 26 as the normal requirement for Game in No Trumps.

Responding to 1 NT with Balanced Hand
As partner has promised 16–18 Points by his opening bid you merely add your Points to his maximum, and if this is short of the

required 26 you pass. Thus you can see that with seven Points or less you pass. There is, however, one exception here. You should raise to 2 NT with only 7 Points if you have a workable five-card suit. The word *workable* is stressed, because it is no good attaching any value to a five-card suit that can never be brought in. For example, you raise 2 NT with:

♠ Q.4   ♡ 9.8.7   ◇ K.J.7.6.3   ♣ J.8.4

but you pass if you hold:

♠ Q.4   ♡ K.8.7   ◇ J.7.6.5.3   ♣ J.8.4

If you hold 8 or 9 Points it depends upon your partner's hand whether your combined holding is enough for game. If he is minimum the Points are insufficient, if he has more you can contract for game. How can you suggest this? By bidding 2 NT.

Now there is another number that you have to remember. It is 33 and is the minimum combined Point Count that produces a small slam. You can readily see that even if your partner holds the maximum 18 Points you must provide at least 15 before there can be any question of a slam. So if you have any number from 10 to 14 you raise happily to 3 NT with no fear of missing anything.

With 15 or 16 Points you are in the same twilight zone that you were with 8 or 9, only this time it is slam, not Game, that is in doubt. Just as you made a tentative bid of 2 NT before, so now you make a tentative bid of 4 NT, which suggests to partner to bid 6 NT with a maximum.

The last number for you to remember is 37, which is the combined Point Count that produces a grand slam. This means that with 17 or 18 Points you bid 6 NT without thought of anything more ambitious.

With 19 or 20 Points you had better content yourself with bidding only 6 NT, in the full knowledge that you may be missing the grand slam. But that is better than losing the substance for the shadow. Methods of dealing with these borderline cases must be left to advanced bidding tactics.

It might be well to summarize the rules.

1. With 7 Points you pass.
   But with 7 Points and a workable five-card suit you bid 2 NT.
2. With 8–9 Points you raise to 2 NT.
3. With 10–14 Points you raise to 3 NT.
4. With 15–16 Points you raise to 4 NT.

5. With 17–20 Points you raise to 6 NT.
   But 19 and 20 Point hands must be treated specially.
6. With more than 20 Points bid 7 NT.

Responding to 2 NT with a Balanced Hand

With the key numbers 26, 33 and 37 in mind you have no difficulty in deciding upon your course of action when your partner opens with a bid of 2 NT. This promises 21 or 22 Points—the problem you have is one of simple subtraction. Here are the rules:

1. With 0–3 Points pass.
2. With 4–10 Points raise to 3 NT.
3. With 11 Points bid 4 NT.
4. With 12–15 Points raise to 6 NT. The 15-Point hand is left to advanced bidding tactics.
5. With 16–18 Points raise to 7 NT.

Responding to 3 NT with a Balanced Hand

Here the number 26 is not applicable, as Game has already been bid. The rules to follow are:

1. With 7 Points raise to 4 NT.
2. With 8–11 Points raise to 6 NT.
   The 11-Point hand is left to advanced bidding tactics.
3. With 12–15 Points raise to 7 NT.

In all cases the possession of a workable five-card suit must be taken into consideration.

Quiz on Chapter 6

Your partner bids 1 NT. What do you bid if you hold:

1. ♠ Q.5.2	♡ J.9.4	◇ J.7.6.3	♣ K.8.6
2. ♠ K.7.4	♡ A.7.4.2	◇ A.Q.J.3	♣ K.6
3. ♠ A.5.2	♡ K.7.4	◇ K.9.3	♣ A.Q.8.4

Your partner bids 2 NT. What do you bid if you hold:

4. ♠ Q.8.6	♡ K.7.5.2	◇ K.8.3	♣ K.5.2
5. ♠ 5.3.2	♡ 8.7.3	◇ A.9.6.2	♣ 6.5.4

7

Suit Bidding

Now that we have seen the Point Count in action in No Trumps bidding, we can turn to suit bidding and try to apply its principles there. As has already been pointed out on page 28, some distributional allowances must be made, when we are dealing with unbalanced hands, otherwise we arrive at the obviously absurd conclusion that the following hands are of equal value:

1.	♠ A.K.9.8.3	2.	♠ A.K.9
	♡ A.K.10.6.4		♡ A.K.10.6
	♢ 8.7		♢ 8.7.4
	♣ 9		♣ 9.8.3

Now it is clear that the first hand is *in attack* far stronger than the second, though they both contain the same number of Points and Defensive Tricks. Wherein does the difference lie? It is in the number of long-card Tricks that can be developed. In the first hand both the Spade and Heart suits can develop two long-card Tricks, giving a total Trick-taking capacity of eight. In the second hand, however, only one long card can be developed in Hearts, which gives a total of five.

How then are we going to assess the higher value of the first hand? Are we to allow something for having a suit of five cards or more? Though this is in fact what we do, it is simpler to fix this allowance through the short-suit remainders, whether they are doubletons, singletons or voids. This is an indirect method of assessment, which resembles the imposition upon motorists of a petrol tax instead of the more direct car tax.

The allowance that has been found reasonably satisfactory is as follows:

For each doubleton	1 Point
For each singleton	2 Points
For each void	3 Points

Now do not imagine that this is a highly accurate assessment, for it is only an approximation. The important thing is that it will

enable you to know when to open the bidding and when to say
No Bid.

Requirements for a bid of one in a suit

When you open the bidding with a suit bid of one, you must observe
three conditions:

1. That you have a biddable suit.
2. That you have at least two Defensive Tricks and 12 Points.
3. That you will bid again if your partner makes a call (other
than No Trumps or a raise of your suit), which is passed by the next
player. Let us now examine these three things. A biddable suit is

(a) Any suit of five or more cards.
(b) Any four-card suit headed by at least the Ace, the King, or
   the Queen and Knave.

With regard to Defensive Tricks it was said on page 27 that in
defence we can count on taking Tricks only with our Aces and
Kings. The two Defensive Tricks must therefore consist of Two
Aces, an Ace-King, an Ace and King-Queen, two King-Queens,
an Ace and two Kings, or four Kings.

The third condition, a guaranteed rebid, plays an important
part in determining what to bid or if to bid. This will be seen later.

Now we have to determine what is the Point range that justifies
an opening suit bid of one. In the case of the No Trumps bid we saw
that 16–18 was the rigid requirement, but in the case of the suit
bid the range is much wider. You will do well at this stage to adopt
12–20 as the limit within which a one bid may fall. At the same time
you will not be a slave to these figures. There are hands on which
you may pass with 12 or even 13 Points, there are hands that have
more than 20 Points which still should be opened with a one bid,
there are even hands that justify a bid with only 11 Points.

Let us take a few hands and see how to deal with them.

1. ♠ A.8.5	2. ♠ K.Q.10.9.7.3
♡ A.7.4.3	♡ 7.6
◇ A.5.2	◇ A.8.7.2
♣ J.9.4	♣ 6

The first hand has 13 Points in actual high cards and has a
biddable four-card suit, so that it satisfies two of the opening
requirements, but the third requirement—a guaranteed rebid—is
not satisfied. If you open with a bid of 1 ♡ you can rebid 1 NT

over your partner's 1 ♠, but you are somewhat embarrassed if he says 2 ◇ or 2 ♣. If you raise the Minor suit bid to three (and there is nothing else you can bid) your partner will expect something a little more robust. Now that you have been shown the difficulties that occur under Condition 3 is not observed we leave the decision to you. Many experts are emphatic that any 13 Points must be opened. On the other hand you will have international players on your side if you decide to pass.

The second hand contains only 12 Points, 9 in high cards and 3 for the distributional allowance, but with a strong rebiddable Spade suit it satisfies Condition 3 and so qualifies for an opening bid of One Spade.

Let us take three other hands:

	3.	4.	5.
♠	A.K.Q.8	A.K.Q.8	A.K.J.2
♡	A.Q.J.7	A.Q.J.7.5	A.K.7.5.3
◇	9.7.6	9.7	9.7
♣	8.2	8.2	8.2

In hand 3 you should open 1 ♠, and over 2 ♣ from partner you rebid 2 ♡. This brings us to Rule 1 applying to hands containing two biddable suits.

With two biddable suits of equal length bid the higher ranking first.

The reason for this is to allow your partner to 'give preference' without increasing the Contract.

On hand 4 you open 1 ♡ and over 2 ♣ rebid 2 ♠. This is Rule 2: *With two biddable suits of unequal length bid the longer first.*

Here we must utter a word of warning. A rebid in a shorter suit of higher rank should only be made when the overall strength of the hand is sufficient, because partner, if forced to give preference for your first suit, must increase the Contract. What this overall strength must be is not reducible to an absolute rule, but you should consider 16 high-card Points as desirable. The hand we are considering is quite strong enough for this 'reverse', as it is called.

Hand 5, however, is not quite strong enough for a reverse. There are two possible methods of dealing with this type.

(a) To open 1 ♡ and rebid 2 ♡, suppressing the Spades altogether.
(b) To open 1 ♠ and rebid 2 ♡.

This tells partner a lie about your hand pattern but it does allow you to mention both suits. You must be guided here by the relative strength of the two suits. With ♠ A.10.7.5 and ♡ A.K.J.6.4 bid and rebid Hearts. If partner cannot bid Spades himself it is unlikely to be the best spot to play. But with the hand in question it is best to open 1 ♠, because the greater strength is concentrated in the shorter suit. From what we have been discussing you can see that before you make a bid you must think out your later course of action. This is what Culbertson called the Principle of Preparedness. Consider these hands:

	6.		7.	
	♠	A.Q.8.4	♠	A.Q.8.4.3
	♡	8.5	♡	8.5
	◇	8.6.4	◇	8
	♣	A.K.9.5	♣	A.K.9.5.4

If on either of these hands you open 1 ♠ and partner replies 2 ♡ or 2 ◇, you are not strong enough to make a 'high reverse' by bidding 3 ♣. The answer to this problem is simple. With a hand of near minimum strength containing biddable Spade and Club suits of equal length, we break our Rule 1 and open with 1 ♣. We may call this the Bid of Convenience. This is employed only in the case of Spades and Clubs. If we change the Spade suits to A.K.Q.8 and A.K.Q.8.4 we can follow the normal procedure of bidding the suits in ranking order.

When a 4—4—4—1 pattern is held you may have three biddable suits. The Bid of Convenience in this case is the suit immediately below the singleton. Let us consider two more hands:

	8.		9.	
	♠	A.Q.7.2	♠	A.Q.7.2
	♡	5	♡	K.J.5.2
	◇	K.Q.8.3	◇	K.Q.8.3
	♣	K.J.5.2	♣	5

On hand 8 you open 1 ◇ and, if partner says 1 ♡, you have an easy rebid of 1 ♠. On hand 9 you open 1 ♠ and are fully prepared to deal with any response your partner makes. There is an exception to this suit below the singleton principle. Let us increase the strength of hand 9 as follows:

♠ A.Q.7.2
♡ A.K.5.2
◇ A.Q.J.3
♣ 5

The high-card strength of this hand makes it difficult for partner to reply at all to a bid of 1 ♠. So the Bid of Convenience must be changed. At first sight it would appear that 1 ◇ is therefore the correct bid, as some authorities recommend. But on deeper consideration it will be found that 1 ♡ is the bid that is most likely to avoid missing a makeable game in Hearts. If partner holds five or even four Hearts to the Queen and a King outside, he would be obliged to pass over 1 ♠ but can raise an opening Heart bid to 2 ♡.

There are other situations that can occur, but you have been shown the main considerations in opening with a suit bid of one.

Quiz on Chapter 7

1. What are the three Conditions governing an opening suit bid of one?

2. What is the rule applying to hands containing two biddable suits of equal length? Is there any exception?

What do you bid on the following:

1. ♠ A.K.Q.4	2. ♠ Q.10.7.5.4	3. ♠ K.8.7.5.3
♡ 8.6.5	♡ A.K.Q.6	♡ 2
◇ A.K.9.7.6	◇ A.4.3	◇ 7.5
♣ 10	♣ 3	♣ A.K.10.8.4

8

Responses to Opening Suit Bids of One

THOUGH the Responder makes every effort to keep the bidding alive in case the Opener has a powerful hand, he is not forced to reply. There are thus four courses of action that are open to the Responder:

A. To pass.
B. To raise the Opener's suit.
C. To bid No Trumps.
D. To bid a new suit.

Let us now consider these four categories and their various subdivisions.

A. The Pass.   0–4 Points

This admits of no variation—for apparent exception see B and C. Opener bids 1 ♠. Responder passes with:

♠ 7.4.2
♡ Q.8.5.3
♢ 9.7.5
♣ Q.8.7

B. The Raise of the Opener's Suit

When you decide to raise your partner's suit, you have to give a new value to your singletons and voids. A moment's reflection will convince you of this. In valuing your own hand the short suit remainders are, as I said before, an indirect assessment of your hand pattern and have no actual Trick value. But in support of your partner, *provided that you have sufficient trumps*, it is clear that your voids and singletons furnish the means for taking Tricks as readily as Aces and Kings. For this reason the Point Count is stepped up, and we reckon a Void = 5 points and a Singleton = 3 Points.

Now we can consider the variations of the raise.

1. The Single Raise.   5–10 Points

1.	♠ 8.6	2.	♠ A.8.5
	♡ Q.7.5.4		♡ K.7.6.3
	♢ 9.3.2		♢ 9.8.4
	♣ Q.10.6.4		♣ K.6.5

In answer to partner's opening 1 ♡, hand 1 represents the minimum —a mere courtesy raise—with only 5 Points. Hand 2 represents the maximum—only the balanced distribution allows a single raise with such high-card strength.

It will be noticed that in each hand the Responder has *four* trumps. This, though highly desirable, is not absolutely essential. There are times when a raise has to be given with only three trumps, but these should be not weaker than Q.3.2 or at a pinch J.3.2. Experience will tell you when to break the rules, but until you have acquired the experience you will be well advised to stick to the rule of four trumps.

2. The Double Raise.   10–12 Points

3.	♠ 7	4.	♠ 7
	♡ 9.7.5.4.2		♡ K.9.7.5
	♢ A.8.5.4		♢ A.8.5.4
	♣ K.5.4		♣ Q.7.6.5

Hand 3, though rated at only 10 Points, is actually worth more because of the five trumps. Compare this with hand 2 and you will see the distributional power of the 5—4—3—1 pattern.

Double raises guarantee at least four trumps, though here again there are times when one might hold only K.Q.2 in trumps, but in that event the Points would be high card not distributional.

Hand 4 is a maximum double raise. Change the ♣ Q to the ♣ K and you should raise to 4 ♡.

3. The Treble Raise.   13–15 Points

	5. ♠ 7	6. ♠ —
	♡ K.8.7.5.3	♡ K.8.7.5.3
	◇ 10.7.6.2	◇ K.10.7
	♣ A.K.5	♣ A.8.7.5.2

Hand 5 is technically a minimum, but again the five trumps and the 5—4—3—1 pattern enhance its value.

Hand 6 has been specially selected. It qualifies as a maximum, but once more it is far stronger than the Point Count makes it out to be. This is to show you that the slave to a Point Count of any sort, even one corrected for distribution, will never achieve the heights. On this hand no really good player would raise to 4 ♡ but would test the slam possibilities by forcing with 3 ♣, or at least bid 2 ♣ followed by 4 ♡, a delayed game raise showing a hand rather too good for a treble raise.

The treble raise guarantees four trumps and hints at five. Its Points are about 10 in high cards and 5 for distribution. If all its 15 Points are in high cards, then clearly the pattern must be balanced and some other bid must be found.

You will see that all six hands have dealt with the raise of a *Major*-suit opening. That is because the ruffing factor that is present in trump Contracts is able to produce the extra Trick that is needed for a Game Contract in Spades or Hearts, but finds it a more difficult task to produce the eleventh Trick that is needed for Game in Diamonds and Clubs. For this reason when your partner opens the bidding with a Minor suit, even if you have good support for it, you are on the look-out for an easier road to Game. If your hand warrants a treble raise you will withhold one raise and bid only three of the Minor suit, so that the 3 NT route to Game is not precluded. Only with the more exotic hand patterns such as the 5—5—3—0, or the 6—4—2—1, or when partner's bidding makes it clear that a NT Contract is impossible, should you settle for the Minor-suit Game.

To illustrate this point let us look back to hand 5, where you raised your partner from 1 ♡ to 4 ♡. Now change the Heart and Diamond suits and assume that partner opens with 1 ◇. You would raise not to 4 ◇ but to 3 ◇.

This covers all the raises of a Major-suit opening, but there is one more in connection with a Minor suit. It is the immediate raise to Game. It shows a freakish distribution, something like a 6—5—1—1, and guarantees five trumps with a strong suggestion of six. It is largely pre-emptive and does not indicate a hand rich in high cards but something like:

7. ♠ 5
♡ 8
◇ K.9.8.6.5.2
♣ A.9.8.6.3

which would be a good raise of 1 ◇ to 5 ◇.

C. No Trumps Responses to the Opening Bid

The responses of 1 NT, 2 NT and 3 NT are all limit bids and are made on balanced hands. There is no distributional allowance for NT responses.

1. 1 NT Response.   6–9 Points

8. ♠ J.7
♡ K.8.6.3
◇ A.6.5
♣ J.7.4.2

Though hand 8 is theoretically the maximum for a 1 NT response it may be better to bid 1 NT even on 10 Points. For example, change ♠ J to ♠ Q, and 1 NT is preferable to an overbid of 2 NT or a 'funny' bid of 2 ♣, over an opening bid of 1 ♠. At the same time you must make every effort to avoid the 1 NT response if some other bid is available. For example, if the opening bid was 1 ◇ the response would be 1 ♡, and the Opener's rebid would give a clearer indication of your eventual destination. At this stage it might be well to glance back at hand 1:

♠ 8.6
♡ Q.7.5.4
◇ 9.3.2
♣ Q.10.6.4

which was a raise of an opening 1 ♡ to 2 ♡. But in response to 1 ♠ you pass.

2. 2 NT Response.   11–12 Points

This is a most abused bid. You must be careful to see that your 11 Points are good ones, that is, that there are strengthening cards like tens and nines. Furthermore you must see that they are in the right place. Let us consider two hands to illustrate this point.

<pre>
    9. ♠ Q.6   10. ♠ A.7.5
       ♡ K.7.3   ♡ K.10.8.3
       ◇ A.7.4.2   ◇ Q.7.4
       ♣ Q.10.8.4   ♣ Q.8.4
</pre>

Hand 9 is a good 2 NT response: all the conditions are right. There is not too much in the Spade suit and the Club Queen is supported by three cards and strong ones at that.

Hand 10, on the contrary, is a bad 2 NT. Too much in Spades, not only in Points but in cards. You might get partner into a losing 3 NT with 4 ♠ a make. The Minor-suit position is far too precarious. If you get away without being caught in one of the minor suits you are just a lucky player. What should you bid on the hand? It is a very difficult question to answer. There is no good bid.

3. 3 NT Response.   13–15 Points

Another much abused bid. If a bare 13 Points are held you should have good intermediates. I make the limit for this bid 13–15 in deference to popular practice, but my personal preference is to reserve this bid to show 15–16 Points with an honour in the Opener's suit. With a 13-Point hand I do not make the *immediate* jump to 3 NT, but find a temporizing bid first.

Here are examples of 3 NT responses to an opening 1 ♠:

<pre>
   11. ♠ Q.6   12. ♠ K.6
       ♡ A.10.5   ♡ A.10.5
       ◇ A.9.7.4   ◇ A.J.7.4
       ♣ K.10.4.3   ♣ K.10.4.3
</pre>

D. Suit Responses to the Opening Bid

Responses in a new suit fall into three main categories.

1. One over One, i.e. a response in a higher-ranking suit.
2. Take Out at the Two Level, i.e. a response in a lower-ranking suit.
3. Jump Take-Out, i.e. two in a higher-ranking suit or Three in a lower-ranking suit.

Let us now consider the three categories.

1. One over One Response. 6–16 Points

	13. ♠ K.10.7.5.3	14. ♠ A.10.9.7.5	15. ♠ A.K.8.4
	♡ 8.4	♡ K.8.4	♡ Q.4.2
	◇ Q.6.5	◇ K.J.6.5	◇ K.J.6
	♣ 10.5.2	♣ 7	♣ K.6.2

On each hand bid 1 ♠ over 1 ♡.

Hand 13 is a near minimum and offers an alternative contract. Prepared to pass any further bid that is not forcing.

Hand 14 is a typical temporizing bid. Prepared to bid for Game as soon as partner's rebid makes clear where the hand should be played.

Hand 15 is a maximum. A forcing bid of 2 ♠ could not be criticized, but the balanced pattern is against it. It is my idea of a good 3 NT response.

2. Take-out at the Two Level. 9–16 Points

Opener bids 1 ♠

	16. ♠ 8.7	17. ♠ A.7.4.2	18. ♠ A.7.4.2
	♡ 9.4.3.	♡ 9.4	♡ 9.4
	◇ A.K.Q.7.4	◇ K.Q.8.7.4	◇ K.Q.8.7.4
	♣ 7.6.5	♣ 7.6.	♣ A.5

Hand 16 is without special interest, but hand 17 shows a very useful method of dealing with the type of hand where you would like to raise your partner to two-and-a-half Spades. You follow the 2 ◇ take-out with a raise of Spades.

Hand 18 is not quite good enough for a forcing take-out, but is ideal for a delayed Game raise. You follow your 2 ◇ take-out with a raise to 4 ♠.

3. Jump Take-out 17 Points and over

This bid is forcing to Game. It is obligatory for the partnership to bid on till a Game Contract is reached, or the opponents have been doubled in a bid that will yield at least an equivalent penalty. The great thing about the forcing take-out is that it allows the partners to bid without fear of being left high and dry. The possibilities of the small or grand slam can be explored without any panic. Thus you can see that the Jump Bid, though it seems to lose a round of bidding, actually facilitates the exchange of information between the partners.

In the early days of Contract Bridge it was held that a forcing take-out guaranteed a fit in your partner's suit. Though support for the Opener's suit is usually present, it is by no means a *sine qua non* if the Responder has a self-supporting suit of his own that is sufficient. The main thing is that before you make a forcing take-out you should have some clear idea of where you are going to play the hand.

19.	♠ K.J.8.6	20.	♠ 4
	♡ A.Q.5		♡ A.7
	◇ A.K.7.2		◇ A.K.Q.J.9.7.3
	♣ 6.3		♣ K.5.2

On both hands it is right to force with 3 ◇, though they are utterly different in their composition. In 19 the force is predicated on the strong support for the Opener's Spade suit. Spades is to be the final Contract. In hand 20 the Responder is not concerned about the singleton in his partner's suit. He has already made up his mind to play in Diamonds, and his main interest is the number of Aces his partner has.

Quiz on Chapter 8

1.	♠ 6	2.	♠ K.10.3	3.	♠ K.7.5
	♡ 9.8.7.5.3		♡ A.10.3		♡ 10.8.7.6
	◇ K.7.3		◇ Q.8.5.4		◇ J.8.7
	♣ A.9.6.4		♣ Q.J.6		♣ 9.7.3

4.	♠ A.Q.J.5	5.	♠ Q.J.9.8.3
	♡ A.10.8.6.3		♡ K.6.4
	◇ K.J.8		◇ A.7.6
	♣ 4		♣ 9.4

Partner opens with 1 ♡. What do you respond on the above hands?

9

Suit Responses to Opening No Trumps

THESE divide simply into three classes, at the two level, three level or four level.

A. Response at the Two Level. 0–7 Points

To take out an opening 1 NT into two of a suit is a weak bid and invites no further bid from the Opener. The hand must be unbalanced, probably with a singleton, and have little in the way of high-card strength. The following is a proper 2 ♠ take-out of partner's 1 NT.

> ♠ 9.8.7.5.3.2
> ♡ 7
> ♢ K.9.5.4
> ♣ 10.3

If you ever hear a player say to you: 'Do you play the weak take-out?' be very suspicious of that remark. It usually means that the player has the disease badly, and that he bids two of a suit over 1 NT on any five cards irrespective of distribution. For example, the following hand

> ♠ Q.8.6.4.3
> ♡ 9.4
> ♢ 8.5.4
> ♣ Q.8.7

is not a proper take-out of 2 ♠. Your partner is likely to do as well in a struggle for seven Tricks as you would for eight.

B. Response at the Three Level. 8 Points and over.

This bid has a wide range, because it may be anything from a distributional try for Game in a Major suit to a full force with a slam in view. You must be quite clear that there are cases where this bid is all right in a Major suit but is not to be used in a Minor. For example:

1.	♠ K.J.10.8.3	2.	♠ 10.8.7
	♡ 4		♡ 4
	♢ 10.8.7		♢ K.J.10.8.3
	♣ A.J.10.6		♣ A.J.10.6

With hand 1 it is right to bid 3 ♠, as 4 ♠ is a sound Contract. With hand 2 you should raise to 3 NT, without losing sleep over the holding of a singleton.

Another hand on which it is quite pointless to bid three of a Minor suit is

> ♠ 7.5
> ♡ 8.6.4
> ♢ A.K.Q.7.4.2
> ♣ 8.7

With this hand 3 NT is the only bid.

Here is a correct use of the Minor-suit three bid. I held this hand in a Gold Cup match. Over my partner's 1 NT I bid 3 ♣ with

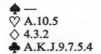

♠ —
♡ A.10.5
◇ 4.3.2
♣ A.K.J.9.7.5.4

and a slam was reached as partner had a maximum.

C. Response at the Four Level.   Seven-card Major Suit

The Points have not been included here because the important thing is the seven-card Major. The Points are somewhere in the region of 5, if contained in the suit, or 7 if outside it. For example, these hands

♠ K.Q.9.7.6.4.3	♠ 10.9.7.6.5.3.2
♡ 6	♡ 6
◇ 7.5.4	◇ K.J.3
♣ 8.3	♣ K.4

are both good 4 ♠ take-outs.

The corresponding Game bid in a Minor suit is not considered here because of its infrequency. Any seven-card suit containing five Points is better played in 3 NT. But if the pattern is really freakish such as 7—5—1—0 the five bid is in order.

Conventional Two Club Take-out

One of the things that was revealed when Contract Bridge ousted Auction and made for greater accuracy in bidding was that eight cards of the trump suit divided four in each hand could develop more Tricks than the 5–3 division. Once this was established a need was felt for some method of finding this 4—4 fit after an opening 1 NT. A conventional 2 ♣ bid Response to 1 NT is now widely employed. The operation of this bid is simple. Opener bids 2 ◇ if he holds no four-card Major suit, with one four-card Major he bids two in that suit, with two four-card Major suits he bids Spades first and may bid Hearts later, if the subsequent bidding warrants it.

Like all new toys this tends to be used too often. There are, of course, times when it works to perfection, but it must be handled with judgment. For instance, if you hold the following:

♠ Q.8.6.5.4.2
♡ J.7.5.4
◇ 7.6
♣ 9

just bid 2 ♠. Any 2 ♣ bid will almost certainly land you in trouble.

You will find it best to employ this bid only when you have some high-card strength, but there is one occasion when you can profitably bid 2 ♣. If your partner says 1 NT and you have something like:

      ♠ Q.7.5.4
      ♡ J.8.5.2
      ◇ Q.9.5.3
      ♣ 8

you are quite safe in bidding 2 ♣, because you can pass *any* response partner makes, whether 2 ♠, 2 ♡ or 2 ◇.

The Stayman Convention

This 2 ♣ take-out of a 1 NT opening bid is generally known as the Stayman convention, although its invention is claimed by more than one player. Today there are some diehards who refuse to employ this convention at rubber Bridge, but there is no good tournament player who does not adopt it as part and parcel of his bidding system. For all that there are many players who do not know how to use it properly. You should be careful, when you are playing with a strange partner, that you both have the same approach to it.

First of all, with the exception of the hand quoted above, do not employ the convention without a fair hand. It would perhaps be helpful to review the reasons for employing it—they are these:

1. To reach a Game contract in a major suit which is divided four in each hand.

2. To reach the best contract—not necessarily at Game level— on unbalanced hands of some 8 to 9 points.

3. To find out where partner's values are, in order to play a slam in the right denomination.

Let us illustrate these:

1.
                    ♠ K.8.6.5
                    ♡ A.10.7.3
                    ◇ Q.4.3
                    ♣ 6.5

♠ 10.2		♠ J.7.4
♡ 8.2	**N**	♡ J.9.5.4
◇ 10.9.7.5	**W E**	◇ A.8.2
♣ A.J.9.7.4	**S**	♣ K.3.2

                    ♠ A.Q.9.3
                    ♡ K.Q.6
                    ◇ KJ.6
                    ♣ Q.10.8

Without Stayman South bids 1 NT, North says 2 NT, and South with more than a minimum says 3 NT. West leads a Club, and the contract goes two down.

With Stayman the bidding is 1 NT—2 ♣—2 ♠—4 ♠, and the contract is unbeatable.

2.

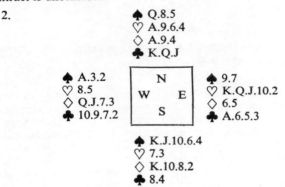

```
                        ♠ Q.8.5
                        ♡ A.9.6.4
                        ♢ A.9.4
                        ♣ K.Q.J
    ♠ A.3.2          ┌──────────┐      ♠ 9.7
    ♡ 8.5            │    N     │      ♡ K.Q.J.10.2
    ♢ Q.J.7.3        │  W   E   │      ♢ 6.5
    ♣ 10.9.7.2       │    S     │      ♣ A.6.5.3
                     └──────────┘
                        ♠ K.J.10.6.4
                        ♡ 7.3
                        ♢ K.10.8.2
                        ♣ 8.4
```

Without Stayman North bids 1 NT, South bids 2♠, and there the bidding ends. With Stayman the bidding sequence is:

N	S
1 NT	2 ♣
2 ♡	2 ♠ (1)
Pass	

(1) This, a new suit introduced, must show five cards.

What is the point of all this? you ask. The result is exactly the same. Certainly, because North has a complete minimum. But let us give North a maximum by exchanging his nine of Diamonds for West's Queen. Now he raises his partner to 4 ♠, and the contract is on ice. But even when North has a maximum, he cannot make 3 NT, because the defence must take four Heart tricks and two Aces.

Here a note of warning must be sounded. There are many hands in which you can make nine tricks in No Trumps but not ten tricks in a 4—4 major suit. Experience will sharpen your judgment and save you from using Stayman on hands which are unsuitable.

3. Now let us consider these hands:

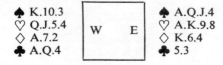

```
    ♠ K.10.3       ┌──────────┐      ♠ A.Q.J.4
    ♡ Q.J.5.4      │          │      ♡ A.K.9.8
    ♢ A.7.2        │  W    E  │      ♢ K.6.4
    ♣ A.Q.4        │          │      ♣ 5.3
                   └──────────┘
```

THE EXPOSED DUMMY

Trumps (here Spades) are on (dummy's) right

THE CUT

The player is cutting the cards for the dealer on his left

Without Stayman West opens the bidding with 1 NT and East, adding his 17 points to his partner's advertised minimum of 16 and arriving at the key number of 33, bids 6 NT, a contract which depends on the Club finesse.

With Stayman we have this sequence:

W	E
1 NT	2♣
2♡	6♡
Pass	

a contract which, with a 3—2 trump break, is unbeatable.

The Stayman convention can also be used over an opening bid of 2 NT, but the procedure is a little different. There are, it is true, some players who employ the conventional response of 3♣ only to ask for a four-card major suit, but the majority of players, and almost all those who compete in tournaments, expect the opener to bid his four-card suits in ascending order, to discover any 4—4 fit. You must realise that now it may be not Game, but slam possibilities that are being investigated. If it should happen that the opener's only four-card suit is Clubs, he is required to rebid 3 NT.

Here is a deal from a pairs tournament of some years ago:

♠ K.Q.7		♠ 6
♡ K.10.6	W E	♡ A.5.4.3
◇ A.K.J		◇ Q.10.5.4
♣ A.J.7.5		♣ K.Q.10.6

Those who did not employ Stayman either failed to reach a slam or played in 6 NT for which there was no play.

The Stayman players bid as follows:

W	E
2 NT	3 ♣
3 NT	6 ♣
Pass	

and twelve tricks were there for the taking.

One final word of advice, When you have agreed to play Stayman with a new partner, make quite sure what procedure you are adopting after 1 NT—2 ♣ when the opener has four cards in each major suit. Some bid Spades first, others Hearts. It does not matter which you do, as long as you both do the same.

Quiz on Chapter 9

In each case partner has opened 1 NT. What do you reply with?

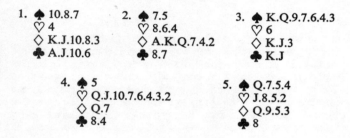

1. ♠ 10.8.7
   ♡ 4
   ◇ K.J.10.8.3
   ♣ A.J.10.6

2. ♠ 7.5
   ♡ 8.6.4
   ◇ A.K.Q.7.4.2
   ♣ 8.7

3. ♠ K.Q.9.7.6.4.3
   ♡ 6
   ◇ K.J.3
   ♣ K.J

4. ♠ 5
   ♡ Q.J.10.7.6.4.3.2
   ◇ Q.7
   ♣ 8.4

5. ♠ Q.7.5.4
   ♡ J.8.5.2
   ◇ Q.9.5.3
   ♣ 8

10

The Opener's Rebids

A. Opening No Trumps receiving No Trumps Response

As HAS already been pointed out in Chapter 6, this is a matter of simple arithmetic. With the key numbers of 26, 33 and 37 in mind, the Opener has only to add his Points to the maximum promised by his partner's bid, and if the sum is short of the key number to pass.

An opening 1 NT raised to 3 NT or 6 NT has no further bid to make. He has limited his hand by bidding 1 NT and can have no justification for any other action.

1. 1 NT raised to 2 NT

Opener passes with 16 Points, and bids 3 NT with 18.

With 17 he has to use his judgment. Good intermediates or a five-card suit will influence him. But generally he should bid the Game, unless there is some specific weakness in the hand such as an unguarded suit.

2. 1 NT raised to 4 NT

Opener is well advised to bid 6 NT only on a maximum, that is on 18.

B. Opening No Trumps receiving Suit Response

1. At the Two Level

This should be passed nine times out of ten. The only excuse for raising a Minor suit take-out is the specific holding of A.K.x or A.Q.x in the suit. This single raise asks partner to bid 3 NT if he holds six to the King or Queen and any additional value. For example:

```
     ♠ A.7.6      ┌─────────┐    ♠ Q.10.4
     ♡ J.10.9.3   │    N    │    ♡ 7.2
     ◇ A.K.5      │ W     E │    ◇ Q.10.8.6.4.3
     ♣ A.Q.8      │    S    │    ♣ 9.3
                  └─────────┘
```

Here West opens 1 NT, East responds with 2 ◇, West rebids 3 ◇ and East obeys instructions and bids 3 NT, as he has six Diamonds and has a Queen on the side.

To raise a Major suit take-out of two to three, the Opener must hold a maximum and exceptional support for the suit. At the same time he does this at his own risk—even the nine-Trick Contract may be in jeopardy if the Responder is weak and the cards lie unfortunately.

2. At the Three Level

If a Major suit raise to four with three or four trumps. With only two trumps bid 3 NT.

If a Minor suit rebid 3 NT with a doubleton, but with three or four of the suit, either raise once or show a suit in which you hold the Ace. This agrees support for the Responder's suit and starts the slam quest. Remember that the bid of three in a Minor must have some meaning, and not be just a lazy way of saying 3 NT.

3. At the Four Level

If a Major suit, there can be no possible reason to bid again.

The Minor suit bid is not considered here.

C. Opening Suit Bid receiving No Trumps Response

1. After a 1 NT Response

Let us assume Opener bids 1 ♡ and hears partner say 1 NT.

The Opener's rebid is governed by two factors, Strength and Shape. It is to be remembered that a 1 NT Response does not demand a rebid from the Opener, as a suit bid does. So the first thing to consider is:

(a) *No Bid*. This denotes a minimum or little more in Points and a balanced hand.

(b) *Two Hearts*. This denotes a near minimum but shows length in the suit.

	1.	♠ 7.4		2.	♠ 7.4
		♡ A.K.Q.7.6			♡ A.J.10.7.5.2
		◇ A.9.5			◇ A.9.5
		♣ 10.8.2			♣ K.6

Hand 1 is a clear pass. Many players make the error of saying 2 ♡ on such a hand, though it should surely play better in 1 NT. On hand 2 you should without any question bid 2 ♡, because it must be a safer Contract.

(c) *Three Hearts*. This denotes a good hand with almost certainly a six-card suit. It is not forcing but is a strong invitation to the Responder to Contract for Game with his maximum of 9 Points.

(d) *Four Hearts*. This denotes a hand only just short of a Two-Bid (see page 72) with about 19 Points and a solid or almost solid suit of at least six cards.

	1.	♠ 7.4		2.	♠ K.5
		♡ K.Q.J.8.7.3			♡ A.K.Q.J.6.3
		◇ A.Q.6			◇ 9.7
		♣ K.7			♣ A.5.2

On hand 1 you rebid 3 ♡ and leave it to your partner, but in view of the solidity of your Hearts in hand 2 you should take the burden off partner and bid the Game.

(e) *Raise 1 NT to 2 NT*. This shows 17–18 Points.

(f) *Raise 1 NT to 3 NT*. This shows 19–20 Points.

1. ♠ Q.6   2. ♠ A.6
    ♡ A.K.J.7.3   ♡ A.K.J.7.3
    ◇ K.9.4   ◇ K.9.4
    ♣ A.J.2   ♣ A.J.2

Hand 1 is a raise to 2 NT, hand 2 to 3 NT.

(*g*) *Rebid of Two in a Lower-ranking Suit.* This shows only a second suit and promises no extra strength. It does not increase the Contract and allows Responder to prefer the first suit at the same level.

            ♠ 8.6
            ♡ A.K.J.7.3
            ◇ 7.4
            ♣ A.Q.7.3

This hand opens 1 ♡ and after the Response of 1 NT rebids 2 ♣. Partner with a doubleton Heart and three or more Clubs passes, but with an equal number gives preference by bidding 2 ♡. *This in no way constitutes a raise.*

(*h*) *Rebid of Two in a Higher-ranking Suit.* This is not a forcing bid, but it necessarily shows additional strength, because preference for the first suit must be given at a higher level. That is, Opener is prepared to play in a nine-Trick Contract.

            ♠ A.K.J.6
            ♡ A.K.J.7.3
            ◇ 8.7
            ♣ 9.5

On this hand Opener bids 1 ♡ and after the response of 1 NT rebids 2 ♠.

(*i*) *Jump Rebid in a new suit.* This is unconditionally forcing to Game. It asks primarily for preference and not for an *unintelligent* NT rebid.

♠ A.K.7.5.3   ♠ Q.8.4
♡ A.Q.J.9.6   ♡ 8.7.4
◇ A.8   ◇ K.9.6
♣ 4   ♣ Q.10.5.3

West bids 1 ♠, and after the response of 1 NT makes a forcing response of 3 ♡. For East to bid 3 NT is unintelligent, and would only be justified by the possession of two doubletons in the Majors.

2. After a 2 NT Response. This is also non-forcing

Let us assume Opener bids 1 ♡ and hears a Response of 2 NT. As in the case of the 1 NT Response the Opener's rebid is governed by the two factors of Strength and Shape.

(*a*) *No Bid.* This shows a balanced minimum.

(*b*) *Three Hearts.* This shows a minimum but a six-card suit, and a desire to play short of Game.

(*c*) *Four Hearts.* This shows the values to try for Game, some 15–16 Points and (probably) a six-card suit.

(*d*) *Three in another suit.* This demands a rebid from the Responder. It offers another suit, and asks primarily for preference. Its strength is unlimited and may be the start of a slam quest.

(*e*) *Three No Trumps.* This shows 14–19 balanced Points.

D. Opening Suit Bid receiving a Raise

Let us assume that the Opener has bid 1 ♡ and hears Response of 2 ♡. The Response shows 5–10 Points, so that Opener says:

1. No Bid with 12–15 Points.

2. Three Hearts with 16–18 Points.

N.B. Some bid at the three level may be made in a lower-ranking suit. Responder must treat this as a game try and bid Game in the first suit if his raise is a good one.

3. Four Hearts with 19 plus Points.

Let us assume Opener has bid 1 ♡ and hears Response of 3 ♡. The Response shows 10–12 Points, so that Opener says:

1. No Bid with a balanced minimum.

2. Four Hearts with anything over a minimum. The mere possession of a six-card suit added to a bare 13 distributional Points is enough.

E. Opening Suit Bid receiving a Response in another Suit

1. One in a higher-ranking suit. This as we have seen shows 6–16 Points

Let us assume that Opener bids 1 ♡ and hears Response of 1 ♠. You are under an obligation to bid again (see p. 35), so it is up to you to find the bid which most accurately describes your Strength and Shape. You can say:

(*a*) One No Trumps

This shows a balanced hand, no good support for Spades, a Heart suit either not rebiddable or not worth rebidding, and no second suit to offer. The Opener has a near-minimum hand such as:

	or	
♠ 6.5.2		♠ 6.5
♡ A.K.9.7		♡ A.K.9.7.2
◇ A.8.5		◇ A.8.5
♣ K.10.7		♣ K.10.7

The first hand is a clear-cut 1 NT, and the balanced nature of the second makes it inadvisable to rebid a not very robust Heart suit. But with a singleton Spade and another small Diamond it is better to rebid 2 ♡.

(b) *Two Hearts*

This shows little more than a minimum, no good support for Spades but a Heart suit worth rebidding, or an unbalanced hand. Opener has a hand such as:

	or	
♠ 6.5		♠ 6
♡ A.K.J.9.7		♡ A.J.9.7.5.2
◇ A.8.5		◇ A.8.5
♣ K.10.7		♣ K.10.7

(c) *Two No Trumps*

(d) *Three No Trumps*

These two bids show the same type of hand with a slight difference in strength. For (c) you require 18, for (d) 20 or a good 19 Points.

♠ 6.5	♠ K.5
♡ A.K.7.4	♡ A.K.7.4
◇ A.K.8.5	◇ A.Q.8
♣ A.9.3	♣ A.10.7.2

On the first hand you rebid 2 NT, on the second 3 NT.

(e) *Two Diamonds*

This does not show any extra strength, but offers a second suit, which partner may pass, if he is weak. The implication is that the hand is unbalanced but it need not be so. Opener should rebid 2 ◇ on the following:

	or	
♠ 6.5		♠ 6.5
♡ A.K.7.4		♡ A.J.9.7.2
◇ A.Q.J.6		◇ A.Q.8.5.4
♣ 8.7.6		♣ 7

It would be as well to insert here (though, of course, it cannot occur in the sequence 1 ♡—1 ♠) the rebid of Two in a higher-ranking suit. If you refer to page 53 you will see that you were told that such a bid must imply something more than a minimum. For example, you open 1 ◇ and after a Response of 1 ♠ you rebid 2 ♡ on a hand such as:

$$
\begin{array}{l}
\spadesuit\ 9.7 \\
\heartsuit\ \text{A.K.Q.8} \\
\diamondsuit\ \text{A.Q.J.7.5} \\
\clubsuit\ 8.2
\end{array}
$$

(f) Three Hearts

This Jump rebid of the Opener's Major suit has caused a lot of bother since the start of Contract. There has never been any clear idea of what this bid implied. Let us apply a little logic to the situation, and see if we cannot define it somewhat more exactly. It must be based on the three things:

1. A self-supporting suit of at least six cards.
2. A Point Count of 16–18.
3. A total of 7 winners or Playing Tricks.

Opener should have a hand such as:

$$
\begin{array}{l}
\spadesuit\ 10.4 \\
\heartsuit\ \text{A.K.J.10.7.3} \\
\diamondsuit\ \text{A.4} \\
\clubsuit\ \text{K.9.7}
\end{array}
$$

(g) Four Hearts

This is a bid that you are unlikely to want. You will realize this after the discussion of the opening two bid, but see page 52.

(h) Two Spades

This shows trump support for partner, preferably four cards in his suit, but there are times when you cannot keep to this ideal. It is when you hold three cards only that you have to use your judgment. The following hands represent raises from 1 ♠ to 2 ♠.

$$
\begin{array}{lll}
\spadesuit\ 8.6.5.3 & & \spadesuit\ \text{K.10.4} \\
\heartsuit\ \text{A.K.J.6} & & \heartsuit\ \text{A.K.J.6} \\
\diamondsuit\ \text{K.9.3} & \text{or} & \diamondsuit\ \text{K.9.8.4} \\
\clubsuit\ \text{Q.7} & & \clubsuit\ 7.5
\end{array}
$$

In the second hand the decision is so close that if you replace the
♢ 4 with the ♣ 4 you should rebid 1 NT.

(i) Three Spades

This promises almost certainly four trumps, and a Point Count of
17–18. If the raise is with A.K.x or K.Q.x of trumps the Points must
be in high cards. Without sufficient *usable* trumps the short suits
cannot be given their full values.

Opener raises a Response of 1 ♠ to 3 ♠ with a hand such as:

> ♠ Q.10.7.3
> ♡ A.K.J.9.6
> ♢ K.J.8
> ♣ 4

(j) Four Spades

This promises at least four trumps and a Count of 19–20. For
example:

> ♠ K.10.7.3
> ♡ A.K.J.9.6
> ♢ A.Q.4
> ♣ 4

(k) Three Diamonds

This bid is known as a Jump Shift and is forcing to Game, and has
slam possibilities if Responder has something more than a minimum.
It may be based on a strong two-suiter, or on a real fit with the
Responder's suit. Its range is 19 Points and over.

> ♠ 7   ♠ K.10.7.3
> ♡ A.K.J.9.8.6   ♡ A.K.J.9.6
> ♢ A.Q.J.9.4   or   ♢ A.K.4
> ♣ 5   ♣ 4

In the first hand Opener is anxious to play for Game in one of
his suits, but he will bid them in such a way as to leave no doubt
that he prefers Hearts. For instance, over a raise to 4 ♢ he will then
bid 4 ♡, clearly showing the extra length in the first suit.

In the second hand the bid of 3 ♢ is not merely to show the
Diamond control but to mark the Club singleton. The next bid will
be a raise to 4 ♠, whatever Responder says.

2. *Two in a lower-ranking suit.* This shows 9–16 Points

The Opener's rebids will be on the same lines as with the one over one Response, but he will remember that the lower limit is 9, not 6, and calculate accordingly.

You saw on page 41 that the Responder, in raising the Opener's suit bid, withheld the treble raise in the case of the Minor suit. The same differentiation must be made by the Opener. Let us illustrate this:

♠ A.K.10.7.5   ♠ A.K.10.7.5
♡ Q.J.3   ♡ A.9
♢ A.9   ♢ Q.J.3
♣ K.J.8   ♣ K.J.8

In the first hand you open 1 ♠ and hear partner say 2 ♡. You raise to 4 ♡. In the second hand you open 1 ♠ and hear partner say 2 ♢. This time you do not bid 4 ♢ but 3 NT.

Quiz on Chapter 10

You open 1 ♠ and Responder says 2 ♣. What do you bid on:

1. ♠ A.J.10.4.3   2. ♠ A.J.10.4.3   3. ♠ A.K.Q.8.7.5
    ♡ K.Q.9.7.6   ♡ K.Q.7   ♡ 7.3
    ♢ 8.4   ♢ A.9.6   ♢ A.8.5
    ♣ 3   ♣ Q.6   ♣ Q.6

You open 1 ♡ and Responder says 1 ♠. What do you bid on:

4. ♠ 7.6   5. ♠ K.Q
    ♡ A.K.J.5.4   ♡ A.K.J.9
    ♢ K.Q.9.7   ♢ K.8.5
    ♣ 10.5   ♣ A.8.7.2

II

The Responder's Rebids

WHEN the Responder has to make a second bid he has already heard two bids from the Opener. He thus should have some idea of the Opener's Strength and Shape, and is in a position to judge whether part-score, Game or Slam is the objective. The crucial decision is his. He must now make quite clear to partner what kind of hand he has—whether poor, fair or good.

We will not deal exhaustively with these Responses, but it will be helpful to consider some specific cases. Let us discuss the Responder's rebid after a one-over-one Response, because the wide margin of 6–16 Points leaves a lot of clarification for the second bid.

Responder's Rebid after a One-over-One Response

Let us take hands 13, 14 and 15 on page 43 and see Responder's rebid.

♠ K.10.7.5.3	♠ A.10.9.7.5	♠ A.K.8.4
♡ 8.4	♡ K.8.4	♡ Q.4.2
◇ Q.6.5	◇ K.J.6.5	◇ K.J.6
♣ 10.5.2	♣ 7	♣ K.6.2

In each case Opener has bid 1 ♡ and Responder has said 1 ♠.

On the first hand Responder has little more than a minimum, and will pass any bid the Opener makes that is not forcing.

On the second hand Responder is only waiting to hear *where* to play the Contract—he already knows that Game is in sight. Here are some possible bidding sequences:

Opener	Responder	Opener	Responder
1. 2 ♡	4 ♡	5. 2 NT	3 ♡
2. 2 or 3 ♠	4 ♠	6. 3 ◇	4 ◇
3. 1 NT	3 ♡ or 3 NT	7. 3 NT	No Bid
4. 2 ◇	4 ♡	8. 2 ♣	3 ◇

In 3 the 3 ♡ bid is forcing, and offers a choice of Contracts. By implication it has only three Hearts, as with four Hearts and the same strength Responder would say 4 ♡.

In 4 Responder is too good even for a Jump Preference and must bid Game.

In 5 again the Heart Contract is offered—the bid cannot be passed.

In 6, in answer to the forcing rebid of the Opener, the Responder just raises the Diamonds once. The small slam is certain and he wants bidding space to try for the grand.

In 7 Responder passes reluctantly, but the slam would not seem to be on in No Trumps.

In 8 it is up to the Responder to force and make life easy for his partner.

On the third hand Responder again knows that Game is certain. Let us take three possible bidding sequences:

Opener	*Responder*
1. 1 NT	3 NT
2. 2 NT	6 NT
3. 4 ♠	6 ♠

All these rebids are matters of simple arithmetic. In the third case it is almost inconceivable that partner has fewer than two Aces, but if you are a cautious player you might like to check for Aces by a conventional bid of 4 NT. This bid will be dealt with in a later chapter.

Trump Support for a Rebid Suit

At this stage it is as well to point out that a suit that has been rebid can be supported with fewer trumps. For example, take the following hand:

♠ 8.4
♡ A.Q.10.9.3
♢ A.7.5
♣ K.6.2

	N		♠ A.K.J.6
W		E	♡ J.5
	S		♢ K.Q.J.6
			♣ 9.8.3

West opens 1 ♡, East responds 1 ♠, and West rebids 2 ♡. East knows that he has the Points to justify a Game and that J.x opposite a rebid suit is adequate trump support, so he says 4♡ without worry.

Respecting the Opener's Sign Off

Opener bids 1 ♡, Responder says 2 NT and Opener bids 3 ♡. By this bid the Opener denies the values to bid either 4 ♡ or 3 NT or to offer any other suit. This is a sign off which Responder must pass. Opener holds something like:

♠ 6.4
♡ K.Q.10.8.7.6
♢ A.4.2
♣ 7.5

Preference Bidding

As the Responder is called upon constantly to give preference, it is essential for you to understand exactly what is implied.

Your partner opens with 1 ♡, you respond with 1 ♠, and partner now says 2 ♣. What should you reply on the following hands:

♠ K.J.8.6.4	♠ K.J.8.6.4
♡ 8.7.5	♡ 9.2
◇ K.7.6	◇ K.7.6
♣ 9.2	♣ 8.7.5

In the first hand you have a minimum and are prepared to pass any bid from partner that is not forcing. But when partner changes the suit you have one more obligation to fulfil, to inform him which of his suits you prefer. You bid 2 ♡. It is important to realize that this indication of preference, as was said before, *in no way constitutes a raise*. It is the equivalent of a pass. We may call this reversion to the first suit bid as Primary Preference.

In the second hand you can show your minimum very easily by saying No Bid. You prefer the second suit so your duty has been done. This we may term Secondary or Passing Preference.

Now let us consider a most important aspect which is called Jump Preference. Opener bids 1 ◇ to which you reply 1 ♠. Opener now bids 2 ♡, and you hold this:

♠ Q.10.9.4.2
♡ 8.6
◇ Q.J.7.6
♣ A.5

A beginner instinctively wants to bid 3 ◇, and is quite horrified at the idea of bidding 4 ◇, which is the correct bid. If you bid 3 ◇ you have given Primary Preference, which is equivalent to saying No Bid. But here you have a definite raise of Diamonds so you show it by a Jump Preference bid.

There are other more subtle examples, but this is enough for you to know at present.

Quiz on Chapter 11

Partner opens 1 ◇ and you respond 1 ♠. Partner then says 2 ♣. What do you say on:

1. ♠ Q.J.10.7.6   2. ♠ Q.J.8.7   3. ♠ Q.J.8.7.2
    ♡ K.10.5   ♡ K.10.5   ♡ 10.8.3
    ◇ 9.4   ◇ K.8.5.3   ◇ 6.4.2
    ♣ 6.4.3   ♣ 7.2   ♣ A.9

Partner opens 1 ◇ and you respond 1 ♡. Partner then says 1 ♠.
What do you say on:

4. ♠ Q.4   5. ♠ J.10.6.5
    ♡ A.Q.7.3   ♡ A.Q.7.3
    ◇ J.5   ◇ 5
    ♣ K.J.10.2   ♣ K.Q.4.3

12

Pre-emptive Bidding

YOU will have seen from the previous chapters that partners arrive
at the best Contract by the intelligent exchange of information. In
much the same way, in time of war, an army depends for its efficiency
on the Intelligence Service. Once the need for Intelligence is accepted
it is a small step to Counter-Intelligence. In Bridge, no less than in
war, we see the same organization, and there are many ways of
misleading or disrupting the opposing lines of communication.
One of the least subtle but most effective methods is the pre-emptive
bid.

Let us see, first of all, what a pre-emptive bid is. It is a bid at the
three, four or five level made on hands that are defensively weak
but can produce a certain number of Playing Tricks in the declared
suit. The sole purpose of these bids is to make it difficult for the
opponents to find out what is the best Contract for their combined
forces. The dealer, or opening bidder, who makes a pre-emptive bid
is in effect saying that in his opinion the enemy have the balance of
power, and, if left to their own devices, will have no difficulty in
bidding and making a Game or even a slam.

Of course, there is no question of any number of Points being
required for a pre-emptive bid. The sole consideration is the number
of Playing Tricks. Mathematically it is worth going down 500
Points to save the first Game. On this basis a player that makes a

pre-emptive bid must be able to win within three tricks if not vulnerable, or two Tricks if vulnerable, of his call. That is to say, he must be able to win six and seven Tricks respectively, if he opens the bidding with a call of Three Spades.

More things have been suffered in the name of pre-emption than in the name of Liberty! Nothing is more satisfying to the man with an inferiority complex than to open with a pre-emptive bid and thereby silence not only his opponents but *his partner*.

There are two cardinal points that you must observe in making a pre-emptive bid:

1. The hand must not be too strong
2. The suit must not be too weak.

I hesitate to generalize, but I should say that any hand with two defensive Tricks is too good for pre-emption. On the other hand, your suit should have solidity (wherever that solidity begins) and not be broken. For example:

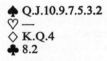

♠ Q.J.10.9.7.5.3.2
♡ —
◇ K.Q.4
♣ 8.2

is a good 3 ♠ bid at Love All, whereas

♠ K.9.7.6.4.3.2
♡ —
◇ A.7.3
♣ 8.4.2

is little short of ridiculous. The weakness of the suit makes it impossible for partner, should he have a good hand, to do anything constructive, and it allows the opponents to defeat you in your Contract, though they cannot make any call of their own.

Now a pre-emptive bid in Spades and, to a lesser degree, in Hearts is quite effective in its attempt to disrupt the enemy, but in the Minor suits the pre-emption loses a good deal of its effectiveness. For this reason, you may find it more to your liking to bid a Minor suit three-bid on a solid suit. Thus to its mild pre-emptive effect against the opponents is added some information that may be vital to your partner.

I would stress the fact that the whole question is one of mood. If you make a pre-emptive bid because you have a certain type of hand or suit you will never present your opponents with the real problems that the unexpected approach may create. Remember, and this is a very important point, that the pre-emptive bid has a curious psychological effect. The opponent, scared stiff of being swindled out of anything, bids with more freedom than he would otherwise. The timid soul becomes aggressive under the spell of the pre-emption. I can recall an occasion, playing against a confirmed underbidder, when with a part-score and a passing partner, I opened with a bid of Three Diamonds though my hand contained five Quick Tricks. Egged on by this bid my vulnerable opponents reached 3 NT, which was a very profitable Contract—for me!

On another occasion, playing in a team of four match, I picked up as dealer:

♠ —
♡ 9.8.4
◇ A.7.3
♣ Q.J.10.8.6.4.3

I decided to open with 1 ♣, instead of the more favoured 3 ♣. When the bidding got round to me again it was clear that the opponents had the balance of the cards. I now bid a psychic 2 ♠, which was overbid by 2 NT on my left. My partner raised to 3 ♠, her only sign of life, and after a double on my right I retreated to 4 ♣. The opponents pressed on to 6 ◇, which I doubled as my partner was on lead. She led (I said she had shown her only sign of life) *a club*! With the 3 ♣ opening I would have had no chance of indicating my desire for a Spade lead.

The pre-emptive bid is most effective before any opposing bid has been made. After your right-hand opponent has opened the bidding you can, of course, crowd the bidding by putting in a high-level bid, but your left-hand opponent is no longer haunted by the fear of being trapped if your partner is very strong. He knows his own partner has the values for an opening bid. For all that, you can certainly cut the lines of communication by throwing a pre-emptive grenade. For instance, after a bid of 1 ♣ on your right, if you hold

♠ 7
♡ K.Q.J.9.8.6.4.3
◇ 8.5
♣ 9.4

you can bid to the limit with 4 ♡. This may have the effect of driving opponents into the wrong suit, of making them bid too much or of making them double you too soon. If you do pre-empt

HOLDING THE HAND

Cards are in numerical order with red and black suits alternating

STACKING THE TRICKS

Declarer has taken five tricks, defenders have taken two and six remain to be decided

go as high as you can, that is, see that your penalty is not out of proportion to the points the opponents could have won at their best Contract.

Defence to Pre-emptive Bids

Naturally, with the vogue for pre-emption, machinery has been manufactured to counteract it. None of the methods are very satisfactory, because the pre-emptive bid, when intelligently employed, can be a very great nuisance. There are times when you have got to give it best. Otherwise you will be like the Poker player who has never been bluffed—a very poor man.

There are three main defences to the opening pre-empt at the three level:

1. Three No Trumps.
2. Four Clubs.
3. Optional Double.

The use of 3 NT as a conventional bid, asking partner to bid his best suit, has one serious disadvantage. It means that the opponents of the pre-emptive bidder can almost never play in 3 NT, though that might be the only Contract. If, for example, you hear an opening bid of 3 ♡ on your right and hold this hand:

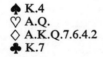

♠ K.4
♡ A.Q.
◇ A.K.Q.7.6.4.2
♣ K.7

it is clear that you can make 3 NT even if partner has a bust, as long as the Diamonds break, whereas 5 ◇ requires assistance. For this reason most good players employ 3 NT as a normal bid over an opposing Three Bid, and adopt the 'Lowest Minor' as the conventional bid for a take-out.

This means that over 3 ◇, 3 ♡ or 3 ♠ the bid for a take-out is 4 ♣, but over 3 ♣ 3 ◇ is used. This has the advantage of keeping the bidding at a lower level. The third expedient, the Optional Double, has a lot to be said for it. It allows the opponents of the pre-emptive bidder to escape a ruinous penalty if they have spoken 'out of turn'. Furthermore, if the pre-emptive bid has been made on a poor suit it allows the partner of the doubler to pass and collect Points when all that he has is in the suit bid. Let us consider the result on the following hand:

C

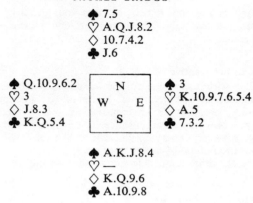

```
                    ♠ 7.5
                    ♡ A.Q.J.8.2
                    ◇ 10.7.4.2
                    ♣ J.6

♠ Q.10.9.6.2    ┌─────────┐      ♠ 3
♡ 3             │    N    │      ♡ K.10.9.7.6.5.4
◇ J.8.3         │ W     E │      ◇ A.5
♣ K.Q.5.4       │    S    │      ♣ 7.3.2
                └─────────┘
                    ♠ A.K.J.8.4
                    ♡ —
                    ◇ K.Q.9.6
                    ♣ A.10.9.8
```

East deals and bids 3 ♡.

No one denies that South has a good hand, but the pre-emptive bid has forced him to contest at a high level. South knows that if it is his partner that has the poor hand they will get a bad result. For all that he has got to make some effort. If he bids 3 NT or 4 ♣ for a take-out he is heading for trouble and will inevitably lose points against good defence. If, on the other hand, he doubles, North will pass and the side will collect a penalty instead of paying one.

Let us change the North and West hands and see if NS still get a good result. The first two bids are the same, but West with powerful trump support and no defence might well boost the bidding with a call of 5 ♡ or even 6 ♡. Over 5 ♡ North goes 5 ♠ and this Contract is cold. But if West does bid 6 ♡ North may be lured into bidding 6 ♠, and cause NS to lose Points on the hand (if EW allow the 6 ♠ bid to stand).

So you see that pre-emption really does make things hard for the opponents. What you, as the opponent of the pre-empter, have got to avoid is 'getting the needle' and making bids which a moment's reflection will show to be absurd. If you think that you are going to find some sure answer to the pre-emptive bid you are sadly mistaken. You cannot expect to get the perfect result every time. There must be times when the pre-emptive bid achieves its object. It is failure to realize this that lands you in trouble.

Of course, it is the timing of a pre-emptive bid that gives it its effectiveness. This is largely a matter of luck. If you open as dealer with 3 ♠ when your partner has a 2 ♣ bid you have clearly not chosen the right moment. But when your opponents have the balance of the cards you have.

Here is a hand played in the Bridge Olympic at Turin. It is a good example of a well-timed pre-emption with co-operation from partner.

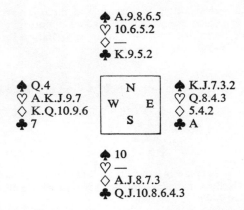

```
                    ♠ A.9.8.6.5
                    ♡ 10.6.5.2
                    ♢ —
                    ♣ K.9.5.2

♠ Q.4                   N          ♠ K.J.7.3.2
♡ A.K.J.9.7        W         E     ♡ Q.8.4.3
♢ K.Q.10.9.6            S          ♢ 5.4.2
♣ 7                                ♣ A

                    ♠ 10
                    ♡ —
                    ♢ A.J.8.7.3
                    ♣ Q.J.10.8.6.4.3
```

Jais and Trezel of the victorious French team scored heavily on this hand against one of the American teams. The bidding was as follows:

S	W	N	E
3 ♣	3 ♡	5 ♣	5 ♡
6 ♣	No	No	Double

After the opening lead of the ♡ K nothing could stop South from making his Contract. Actually a trump lead sets the Contract, but the American West can hardly be censured for not leading his singleton.

Let us now dispassionately analyse the result of this hand. The French bidding achieved a fine result because South found his partner with exactly the right type of hand and because North added to the opponents' difficulties by a further jump in the bidding. East is in the position of not knowing whether the opponents are out of their depth or not. It is hard to tell who is attacking and who is defending. Suppose we change the North and West hands. Now is the opening 3 ♣ bid going to benefit N and S? Will they be likely to finish in their correct Contract of 5 ♢?

Remember then that a pre-emptive bid depends for its effectiveness on the following:

1. Restriction of opponents' bidding space.
2. Good Timing.
3. Psychological reaction of the opponents.

Nothing can be done about the first two of these. The real swings come from the third factor. If you are the opponent of the pre-empter don't be misled by doubt, fear or irritation into actions which you are most likely to regret.

Quiz on Chapter 12

On which of the following three hands is a bid of 3 ♠ in order?

1. ♠ K.9.7.6.4.3.2
   ♡ 4
   ◇ A.8
   ♣ 9.6.5

2. ♠ Q.J.10.9.7.5.3.2
   ♡ 4
   ◇ A.8
   ♣ 9.6

3. ♠ K.Q.9.8.6.4.3
   ♡ 4
   ◇ A.7.5
   ♣ 9.6

What should be bid on any hand not suitable for a pre-emptive bid?

4. What is the chief objection to 3 NT as a take-out over an opposing three bid?

5. Your partner North, at Game to EW, deals and bids 3 ♡ and East passes. What do you say with ♠ 8.6.5 ♡ K.10.7.6.4.2 ◇ 9.7.3 ♣ 8?

13

Two Bids

WITH the advent of Contract Bridge and its requirement that Games and Slams had to be bid to be scored, the need was felt for a bid that would allow a player with an overwhelmingly strong hand to demand that the bidding be kept open until at least Game had been reached. This made it easier to find the best Contract. Without such a Forcing Bid the Opener would be obliged to shut his eyes and guess. For example, a player holding

♠ A.K.J.9.8.4
♡ A.K.J.8.5
◇ A.6
♣ —

would have no alternative but to bid 4 ♠, or 6 ♠ if he felt like it.
Suppose that his partner held

♠ 3
♡ Q.9.7.6.2
◊ K.10.7.4
♣ 8.6.5

You can see that 7 ♡ is almost a lay-down, while even 6 ♠ is in
doubt.

In the Culbertson system a two bid in any suit is forcing to
Game. The so-called 'negative' Response is 2 NT. This has a certain
disadvantage, if the final contract is 3 NT, because the strong hand
is exposed on the table. Not only does this allow the opening lead
to be *through* the strength, but it makes it easier for the defence to
find the correct line to adopt.

Of recent years, certainly in England, there has been a swing
towards the conventional 2 ♣ bid as the only forcing-to-Game call.
This call is purely artificial and does not depend on any specific
holding in the Club suit. It merely announces a hand of five Quick
Tricks and sufficient Playing Tricks to make a Game likely with
almost no support from partner. The negative response is 2 ◊. This
call indicates that the Responder has no values for a positive
Response. It does not necessarily imply a worthless hand, though,
of course, that may be the case, but it denies

1. An Ace and a King.
2. A King and a King-Queen.
3. Three Kings.

The first Response is concerned primarily with high-card strength.
The Opener who has announced a hand of Game-going proportions
is anxious to hear whether his partner has the values for a positive
Response or not. After the Response, whether positive or negative,
the Opener now shows his suit. In other words he shows *where* his
strength lies. The Responder does the same, and either raises the
Opener's suit or bids one of his own. It will be helpful to consider
the bidding of two hands, one receiving a positive, one a negative
Response.

1. ♠ A.K.J.10.4   ♠ Q.7.3
   ♡ A.K.Q.J   ♡ 6.5
   ◊ A.Q.J   ◊ K.9.5
   ♣ Q   ♣ A.J.10.7.2

The bidding between West and East is as follows (NS are silent):

West	East
2 ♣ (a)	3 ♣ (b)
3 ♠ (c)	4 ♠ (d)
4 NT (e)	5 ◇ (or 6 ♣) (f)
7 ♠ (g)	—

(a) Conventional bid which says: I have 5 Quick Tricks. I have all but Game in my own hand.

(b) A positive Response. I have one of the three requirements (see above) for a positive Response, and I have a biddable Club suit.

(c) I have a Spade suit.

(d) I have trump support for Spades.

(e) Conventional bid which says: How many Aces have you?

(f) Conventional bids. 5 ◇ is a Blackwood Response and denotes the holding of one Ace. 6 ♣ is a Culbertson Response and denotes the holding of the Ace of Clubs.

(g) West now knows that partner holds ◇ K and ♣ A, or ♣ A.K and can count 13 tricks.

N.B. The bid of 4 NT and the responses in (e) and (f) will be fully explained in the chapter on slam bidding.

2.	♠ A.K.Q.7.5	♠ 9.4
	♡ A.K.Q.4.3	♡ J.7.5.2
	◇ A.6	◇ K.9.7.3
	♣ 8	♣ 7.4.2

This time the bidding is as follows:

West	East
2 ♣	2 ◇ (a)
2 ♠ (b)	2 NT (c)
3 ♡ (d)	4 ♡ (e)
5 ◇ (f)	6 ◇ (g)
6 ♡ (h)	—

(a) I have not got a positive Response.

(b) I have a Spade suit.

(c) Sorry. I cannot support it.

(d) I also have a Heart suit.

(e) That I can support.

(f) I have the Ace of Diamonds—can you help?

(*g*) Yes, I have the King.

(*h*) In that case 6 ♡ must be a good thing.

N.B. West's bid of 5 ◇ is a Cue bid and will be fully explained in the chapter on slam bidding.

Not every 2 ♣ bid results in a slam, but these two have been put in to show you two things. First, how smoothly the bidding proceeds under the protection of the 2 ♣ bid which ensures the reaching of the Game level, and, secondly, how little assistance a strongly distributional 2 ♣ bid requires. Anyhow it is time for you to have slams in your consciousness!

In Chapter 5, you may remember, it was said that the method adopted by many experts today to deal with balanced hands of 23 and 24 Points is to open with a 2 ♣ bid and to rebid 2 NT over a 2 ◇ response. This is the only sequence which can be dropped short of Game. Responder with fewer than four Points may pass. Let us see such a 2 ♣ bid in operation. West bids 2 ♣ and East replies 2 ◇ on:

♠ A.Q.7	♠ J.4
♡ A.K.5	♡ Q.9.7.6
◇ A.J.7	◇ 9.8.4.3
♣ K.Q.9.8	♣ J.6.2

On the second round West bids 2 NT and East with four Points raises to 3 NT. If we remove East's Queen of Hearts and substitute a small card, East passes 2 NT. I repeat, this is the only case where the 2 ♣ bid is not forcing to Game.

With the bid of 2 ♣ reserved for five Quick Trick hands, the bids of 2 ♠, 2 ♡ and 2 ◇ are released to describe hands whose power is dependent upon distribution rather than high cards. This is the great contribution of Acol to modern bidding. The Acol Two Bid is forcing for one round, and announces a hand of great playing strength, of at least eight Playing Tricks, in the declared suit. At this stage it might be as well to decide what honour strength is required for this bid. Obviously it must be less than five Quick Tricks, otherwise it would qualify for a 2 ♣ bid. Clearly too, its honour strength cannot be confined to the trump suit. For example, the following hand

♠ 7.4
♡ A.K.Q.J.9.8.4.3
◇ 7
♣ 9.4

does not measure up to the required standard. Its defensive value is so small that it must be opened as a pre-emptive bid of 4 ♡. Somewhere between these limits lies the honour strength requisite. It is hard to lay down an absolute rule, but I would suggest that you take $3\frac{1}{2}$–4 Quick Tricks as your basis. The following hands

both qualify as opening bids of 2 ♡.

One word of warning should be uttered here. The second of these hands is a lovely hand to hold in attack, but do not be disappointed if the opponents make eleven Tricks in Spades against you.

In addition to the one-suited hand the two bid may be used with a strong two-suiter.

Here is such a hand:

♠ A.K.J.6.5.2
♡ A.Q.J.8.5
◇ 7
♣ 6

Responses to the Two Bid

1. The negative Response is 2 NT, corresponding to 2 ◇ over 2 ♣.

2. A single raise of Opener's suit shows trump support and an Ace. This is an unlimited bid, and there is no need to give any more than a single raise if you have trump support, no matter what your strength. I regard this early raise in partner's suit as most important. Many a grand slam has been missed because Opener was not sure about the Queen of trumps.

3. A double raise denotes good trump support, some honour strength but no Ace or void.

4. To bid a suit of his own the Responder needs a reasonable suit and not less than one Quick Trick.

5. A response of 3 NT shows something like a 2 NT Response to a one bid, *without an Ace*.

Further Action by the Opener

After a negative Response the Opener, with a one-suited hand containing the bare eight winners, rebids 3 ♠ (or 3 ♡), which the

Responder may pass. If, however, he has nine winners he bids for Game. If he has two suits he bids three in the second, unless his hand is so strong that it warrants a jump bid. The Responder may pass a simple change of suit but only with a worthless hand.

There is plenty of scope for intelligence in the rebids with really powerful hands. It is possible for the Opener to paint a picture of his hand for the Responder and so make it the easiest thing in the world for him to supply the missing pieces. For example, West opens 2 ♠ with the following

♠ A.K.J.8.6.4.3	♠ Q
♡ —	♡ 9.7.6.4.2
◇ —	◇ 8.6.5.3.2
♣ A.Q.J.10.5.4	♣ K.6

and East responds with 2 NT. West now rebids with a call of 5 ♣. This unnecessary jump shows partner clearly that he has eleven cold Tricks and is only interested in high honours in the suits he has mentioned. Armed with this information East has no difficulty in bidding 7 ♠. He holds the two key cards, and raises once for each of them.

If you hold a single-suited hand in one of the Minors, you must be careful to hold an extra winner, because of the need to win eleven Tricks for Game.

Quiz on Chapter 13

What do you open on the following:

1. ♠ A.K.Q.5	2. ♠ A.K.Q.8.5.4.2	3. ♠ A.Q.4.3
♡ A.Q.J.7.3	♡ A.K.Q.J.8.7	♡ A.K.6.5
◇ 8	◇ —	◇ 7.6
♣ A.K.9	♣ —	♣ A.K.3

Your partner opens 2 ♠. What do you reply with:

4. ♠ Q.8.5	5. ♠ Q.10.6.4
♡ A.6	♡ 7.5.3.2
◇ 9.7.6.4	◇ K.8.6
♣ A.8.6.3	♣ K.7

14

Slam Bidding

IN THE days of Auction Bridge you could play unopposed in a Contract of 1 ♠, find your partner with most of the cards you were missing and make either twelve or thirteen Tricks. For this you received 50 or 100 Points, a wholly undeserved bonus for making a small or grand slam. Nowadays, you have to bid your slams as well as make them, before you can score the attractive premiums that they bring with them.

If you decide, from a sense of inferiority, that you will not try to bid for slams, then you condemn yourself to three things. First, you will miss a tremendous lot of fun, secondly, you will never be anything but a really bad player, and thirdly you will lose even more than otherwise. If your opponents get a premium for their good cards and you do not, it is clear that you are not working on a sound economic basis.

There are three methods of slam bidding open to you:

1. The Direct Method.
2. Cue Bidding.
3. The Four No Trumps Convention.

No good player confines himself to any one of these methods, but he uses them all according to the requirements of the moment. Now it needs a lot of experience before you become really proficient at slam bidding, but it will be helpful to you if we consider the three methods and the right occasions for using them.

We have already learned that 33 Points will in most cases offer a good play for twelve Tricks, and 37 Points for thirteen Tricks. If your Points added to the minimum shown by partner's bid add up to 33 or more, you can just bid the small slam. You will find this method most effective in No Trumps bidding. For example, you hold

♠ K.Q.5
♡ A.9.7.4
◇ K.8
♣ A.Q.9.3

74

and hear your partner open the bidding with 1 NT. There is no need to waste time—just bid 6 NT. You have 34 Points between you and the slam should be safely delivered.

It is, of course, possible to employ the same method in suit slams, but you must not forget that the distributional count, though it may indicate twelve winners, may fail to indicate that there are two quick losers. For that reason, it is better to check for Aces or distributional controls by one of the other two methods. For all that, if you are preparing to embark upon a risky slam, you will have a much better chance of making it by the direct method, because your bidding will not have disclosed to the defence exactly where your weakness lies. With the following hand

♠ 8
♡ A.K.8.7.5
♢ K.Q.6
♣ A.Q.10.4

if your opening bid of 1 ♡ is raised to 3 ♡ by partner you could just say 6 ♡. He is unlikely to have all you need for the grand slam, but you will be sure to have a good play for twelve Tricks.

We come now to cue bidding. This method is exploratory. It is an attempt to find out if partner's values are in the right place. You were shown an example of this in the last chapter, on page 70, where West bid 5 ♢ over his partner's 4 ♡. But here is another hand which contains a cue bid:

♠ A.K.8.6.4	♠ J.3
♡ A.J.9.2	♡ Q.8
♢ Q.7.5	♢ A.K.J.9.8.4
♣ 6	♣ A.Q.5

The bidding goes as follows:

W	E
1 ♠	3 ♢
3 ♡	3 NT
4 ♢	5 ♣
6 ♢	—

West knows after East's bid of 3 NT that he must have a good Diamond suit. He has not been able to support either of the Major suits, nor has he a Club suit to bid. West therefore issues a slam invitation by bidding 4 ♢. East accepts the slam suggestion, and shows the Ace of Clubs. This allows West to bid 5 ♡ if he happens to have the King of Hearts, and so pave the way to the grand slam.

The third method is the Four No Trumps convention. It is employed when a player is concerned chiefly with the number of Aces and Kings held by his partner. This convention has two forms:

1. The Culbertson Four No Trumps.
2. The Blackwood Four No Trumps.

Of the two the first is somewhat more complicated. It is as well to give a brief explanation of its functioning, but the player is advised to gain some experience before he adopts this Four No Trumps as his conventional bid.

After Game has been reached, or after strong bidding by either partner, you may bid 4 NT with the following qualifications, either:

1. Three Aces   or
2. Two Aces, and a King of any suit bid by you or your partner. The responses to the 4 NT are strictly defined.

(*a*) With two Aces
    With one Ace and Kings of *all* suits bid by the ⎫ 5 NT
partnership   ⎬
                                                     ⎭
(*b*) With one Ace in an unbid suit   5 of that suit
(*c*) With one Ace in a bid suit   6 in the best trump suit
(*d*) With no Ace   5 in the lowest-ranking bid suit.

If the 4 NT bidder *after a sign off* bids 5 NT he shows that he holds all four Aces.

We now come to the Blackwood, which is widely played, even by experienced players, because of its greater simplicity. The purpose of this convention is again to find out the Aces and Kings held. But, unlike the Culbertson convention, the bid of 4 NT does not guarantee any specific holding—it is purely asking for information. The responses to 4 NT are as follows:

1. With no Ace (*or with four Aces*)   5 ♣
2. With one Ace   5 ♢
3. With two Aces   5 ♡
4. With three Aces   5 ♠

If the 4 NT bidder now makes a 5 NT bid he is asking the Responder to show Kings on the same scale, except that 6 ♣ indicates no King and 6 NT indicates four Kings.

Let us now see how the two systems operate on the same hand.

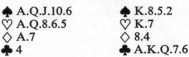

♠ A.Q.J.10.6   ♠ K.8.5.2
♡ A.Q.8.6.5   ♡ K.7
◇ A.7   ◇ 8.4
♣ 4   ♣ A.K.Q.7.6

The bidding goes:

	W	E		W	E
	1 ♠	3 ♣		1 ♠	3 ♣
Culbertson	3 ♡	3 ♠	Blackwood	3 ♡	3 ♠
	4 NT	5 NT		4 NT	5 ◇
	7 ♠	—		5 NT	6 ♠
				?	

After the Culbertson 4 NT, the response of 5 NT shows one Ace and the Kings of all the bid suits. So it is easy for West to bid the grand slam. After the Blackwood 5 NT, however, West knows that East has three Kings but he does not know which they are. If the vital Heart King is missing he cannot bid seven. This does not mean that the Blackwood 4 NT should not have been used. The mistake was in following it with a 5 NT bid. It was possible to make a more intelligent bid. Over East's 5 ◇ West should have bid 6 ◇, which would have allowed East to bid 6 ♡. This would have made the grand slam easy to bid. Thus you see that the Blackwood must not be used as a blunt instrument to force your way to a slam. It must be employed only when the specific information that it is designed to give is what you want. If it cannot give you what you want you must look to some other means for reaching your slam.

The beginner is advised to use Blackwood for keeping him out of an unmakeable slam, rather than for bludgeoning his way into it. For example:

♠ A.K.J.6.4   ♠ Q.8.7.5.3
♡ 8   N   ♡ K.Q
◇ A.9.5   W   E   ◇ K.10.8.6.2
♣ K.Q.J.6   S   ♣ 4

Here the bidding goes:

W	E
1 ♠	3 ♠
4 NT	5 ♣
5 ♠	—

The knowledge that East has no Ace keeps the partnership out of all trouble and the Declarer plays happily in 5 ♠.

It is as well to point out early that great care must be exercised when the agreed trump suit is Clubs. If you bid 4 NT, hoping for a 5 ♡ Response, and receive 5 ♢ instead, you are already committed to a small slam because Clubs is a lower-ranking suit.

There is a point that must be appreciated—the mathematical odds involved in slam bidding. Let us first of all consider the small slam.

If you are not vulnerable you get an extra 500 Points for bidding and making a small slam. If you bid the slam and go down one trick you lose 50 Points plus the value of the first Game which is reckoned at 300. In addition you lose 50 for one undoubled (usually) under-trick and 30 for one overtrick, as well as the 120 for the Trick score. This adds up to 500 Points, so that in bidding a small slam when not vulnerable you are risking 500 to gain 500, which is clearly an even-money proposition. From this it follows that you must not accept worse 'playing' odds than this. To make this more readily understood, let us consider a slam that depends upon a successful finesse (see page 97). If you hold Ace and Queen of a suit, it is obviously a 50–50 chance whether the right-hand or left-hand opponent holds the King. In one case you are defeated, in the other you bring home the slam. But if your slam depends upon two of such even-money chances the odds have worsened to 3–1 against. In this case you would be wrong to bid the slam.

We need not go into the figures involved when you are vul-nerable. It is enough to say that the same even-money chance is offered. We can thus arrive at a positive conclusion.

A small slam should be bid whenever the twelfth Trick depends upon a finesse. It should be pointed out that in a small slam Contract the expected finesse may be avoided by Elimination or Squeeze, so that *a good player* is getting better than the even-money chance.

When it is a question of a grand slam, however, the chances are quite different. If you bid a vulnerable grand slam and go down one you lose 100 + 180 + 750 + 500 = 1530, which represents one undertrick, six Trick Points, vulnerable small slam bonus, and Rubber Points. If you make your grand slam you score 2210, so that you are risking 1530 to gain 680. Clearly you cannot accept a finesse as a reasonable bet. The same is true when not vulnerable. Therefore, our conclusion is that *A grand slam to be a justifiable risk must be 3—1 on.*

In pre-war days, when aggregate scoring was used in Gold Cup and other team-of-four matches, I used to tell my team never to bid a grand slam unless they could count the thirteen Tricks. I broke this rule once myself. I held six Spades to the A.K.Q and knew that my partner had at least three. I could count thirteen

Tricks if the Spades broke. I bid 7 ♠ and found all four to the Knave on my left. Of course, I was getting enormous odds, but I still went down!

If you bid a slam and go down or if you fail to bid a slam that is cold, don't be discouraged. The experts who have been playing for years do just that. Some slams are very easy to bid, others are difficult, and require the right bid made at the right time.

Here, finally, is a hand which occurred in an international match.

♠ K.Q.5	♠ A.J.9.8.3
♡ 7	♡ 9.6.2
◇ A.K.9.4	◇ 10.6
♣ K.Q.J.7.5	♣ A.8.2

My partner West opened with 1 ♣, to which I replied with 1 ♠. West now bid 3 ◇ unconditionally forcing to Game, and I said 3 ♠. Partner now bid 4 ♠. Now it was I with the weaker hand that made the slam try with a bid of 5 ♣. You see, my partner's bidding had marked him with a singleton Heart. All that stopped me from bidding 6 ♠ right away was the fear that the trump Queen might be missing. So my bid of 5 ♣ expressed interest in the slam. Knowing I held the Club Ace, partner could now bid the small slam with confidence. This slam was bid without any 4 NT convention. It was the result of inferences correctly drawn.

Quiz on Chapter 14

In each case you are playing Blackwood.

1. Your partner bids 4 NT. What do you reply if you hold two Aces?

2. You hold:

♠ A.K.9.7.5.2
♡ 6
◇ A.K.Q.8.6
♣ 4

You open the bidding with 2 ♠ and partner replies with 3 ♠.
(a) What do you bid now? (b) Why?

3. You hold:

♠ K.J.6.3
♡ A.Q.9.7.6
◇ A.K.4
♣ 8

You open the bidding with 1 ♡ and partner says 1 ♠.
(a) What do you bid now? (b) Why?

15

Defensive Bidding

IN ALL the bidding that we have so far discussed the Defending Side has preserved strict silence. You will remember that earlier in the book we defined the Defending Side as the opponents of the Declarer. That referred to the period of play. But we can also apply this term Defender during the bidding, to denote the player who makes a positive bid after one of his opponents has opened the bidding. It may so happen that the Defending Bidder and his partner obtain the Contract and thus become the Declaring Side.

In no department of the game is there greater need of judgment and level-headed calculation. I would go so far as to say:

1. It is at the lower levels of defensive bidding that the weak player loses heavily.

2. It is at the higher levels of competitive bidding that the good player, even the very good player, shows the cloven hoof.

After an opponent has opened the bidding, you must have some good reason before you decide to contest with a bid of your own. What good reasons are there? They can be divided into two main classes, Obstructive and Constructive.

Obstructive

1. To disrupt the opponents' bidding. For example, after an opening bid of 1 ♣ on your right you can make things awkward by pre-empting with 4 ♡ on:

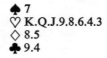

♠ 7
♡ K.Q.J.9.8.6.4.3
♢ 8.5
♣ 9.4

This hand was mentioned on page 64, and the reader is advised to study the comments once more.

2. To keep the opponents from their best Contract. For instance, holding nothing but ♡ A.K.Q.J, you should bid 1 ♡ over an opening 1 ♣ or 1 ♢. If you do not your opponents may bid and make 3 NT, as even if your partner leads a Heart you have only four

Tricks to make. If you bid, however, they will be certain to place you with five of your suit, and so be kept out of their only makeable game.

3. To prevent the opponents from making their Contract by suggesting to partner the correct lead to make.

4. To suggest to partner a suit in which it may be profitable to sacrifice against the opposing Contract.

Constructive

1. To prepare the way for a part-score, Game, or even slam Contract.

2. To lay the foundation for a Penalty Double if the opponents bid too high.

Minimum Overbids

A minimum overbid is made at the one level if your suit outranks that of the Opener, at the two level if it does not. Whichever it is, it must be based upon the factor of safety. The value of a game is approximately 500 Points, so that an overbid must not risk more than 500 Points. This means that you must be able to win within three Tricks of your Contract, if not vulnerable, and within two Tricks if you are vulnerable

It is clear, then, that an overcall should not be based upon Points primarily, but upon Playing Tricks. Furthermore, you should have at least five cards in the suit. You will at once point out that earlier in this chapter I advocated an overbid of 1 ♥ holding only A.K.Q.J. That is true—the possession of the four top honours makes the danger of being doubled in a one bid very small. This is exceptional, and you should make sure that you have five cards in your suit.

Overbids at the one level

Your right-hand opponent opens the bidding with 1 ♥. You may overbid 1 ♠ with

♠ A.Q.J.9.5   ♥ K.6   ♦ 10.8.7.3   ♣ 7.4

because you have a five-card suit and you should take five Tricks altogether.

Overbids at the two level

This is where great care has to be exercised. This is the overbid that costs the weak player thousands of Points annually. The reason is that he does not appreciate the position properly, and overbids on the wrong type of hand. Let me make a point that is not sufficiently treated in the text books. *When you overbid at the two level you are giving your left-hand opponent an extra bid.* Let us illustrate:

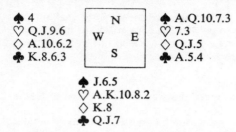

```
                        ♠ 4
                        ♡ Q.J.9.6          ♠ A.Q.10.7.3
                        ◇ A.10.6.2         ♡ 7.3
                        ♣ K.8.6.3          ◇ Q.J.5
                                           ♣ A.5.4

                        ♠ J.6.5
                        ♡ A.K.10.8.2
                        ◇ K.8
                        ♣ Q.J.7
```

The North hand is omitted. If East opens with 1 ♠ and you pass, West has a difficult bid. The opponents may, or may not, bid 3 NT—they may not make it if they do. But if you bid 2 ♡, West has no problem—he just doubles. You will lose 700. It is no good looking pathetically at partner and saying, 'I had 14 Points.' That is exactly why your bid was bad. You had Points without a good enough suit. If your hand had been

    ♠ K.5   ♡ K.Q.J.10.8.2   ◇ 8.7.4   ♣ 8.7

you would have had only 9 Points but a very much better call of 2 ♡, for with this hand any 300 or 500 loss would not have been in vain.

Remember, then, that in your overcalls you must be concerned not so much with points as with Playing Tricks, based on a robust suit.

No Trumps Overbids

This is no problem—the same conditions apply as for an opening 1 NT, except that a guard in the opener's suit is, of course, obligatory. The reader would be well advised to have a double guard in the opposing suit and overbid 1 NT over 1 ♠ on

    ♠ K.10.8.6   ♡ A.10.2   ◇ K.Q.J.4   ♣ K.5

It is also possible to overbid an opening 1 ♠ with 2 NT on a hand such as

    ♠ A.J.10   ♡ A.Q.   ◇ A.K.5.4   ♣ K.8.3.2

which has the qualifications for an opening 2 NT, with a double guard in the opponents' suit, but a 3 NT overbid will be a strategic bid on a hand like

    ♠ K.5   ♡ A.4   ◇ A.K.Q.8.6.5.2   ♣ K.8

Informatory (Take-out) Double

First of all we must be quite clear when a Double is for a take-out and when it is for penalties. An informatory Double must comply with the following conditions:

1. It must be the doubler's first opportunity to double.

2. The doubler's partner must have made no positive bid, Double or Re-double.

3. The opposing bid must be for fewer than nine Tricks. (But see Pre-emptive Bidding.)

4. The opposing bid must be in a suit. (But see Responses to Informatory Double.)

It may be as well to examine a few cases:

	W	N	E	S
(a)	1 ♠	Double	No Bid	?
(b)	1 ♠	No Bid	2 ◇	No Bid
	2 ♠	Double	No Bid	?
(c)		1 ♡	No Bid	1 ♠
	2 ◇	Double	No Bid	?

What should you, South, do in each case? In (a) the Double is clearly informatory as all four conditions are observed. In (b) the Double is for penalties as partner has not doubled at his first opportunity. In (c) the Double is for penalties as you have made a positive bid.

Requirements for an Informatory Double

1. Points. From 13 high-card points upwards.

2. Pattern. Ideally 5—4—4—0 or 4—4—4—1 with the void or singleton in the opponent's suit. The ability to provide four-card support for whatever suit your partner bids is *all-important*.

3. Major Suit Support. If the opposing bid is in a Major suit, it is *de rigueur* to have good support for the other.

4. Preparedness. You must not lose sight of the fact that partner may have a complete Yarborough. If, then, any response on his part can land you in a disastrous Penalty Double, you are not prepared to make an Informatory Double.

Let us now look at some examples:

I.   ♠ 7   This is a good Double of an opposing 1 ♠,
    ♡ A.J.8.3   as you have 14 Points and can provide four-
    ◇ K.J.10.6   card support for any suit.
    ♣ A.J.7.6

II. ♠ 9.7.6.5.3   The exceptional 5—4—4—0 pattern makes
     ♡ —   this an excellent Double of 1 ♡, and we
     ◇ A.K.10.4   break Rule I with only 12 Points.
     ♣ K.Q.9.6

III. ♠ K.8.9.4   This breaks Rule 2 as the pattern is 5—4—
     ♡ A.K.Q.6.4   3—1, but it is a good Double of 1 ◇. If
     ◇ 6   partner bids 2 ♣ we bid 2 ♡, showing five
     ♣ A.7.5   Hearts and a hand too good for a mere over-
                   bid.

IV. ♠ A.6   This breaks Rules 2 and 3 but is still a good
     ♡ 7   Double of 1 ♡. Over the expected Spade
     ◇ A.K.J.10.7 response we bid Diamonds, again showing
     ♣ K.Q.10.9.4 a hand too good for a mere overbid.

V.   ♠ 8.5.2   This hand has 15 Points but it is not an In-
     ♡ A.7   formatory Double. It cannot cope with a
     ◇ A.Q.7.6   Response of 2 ♡. It breaks Rule 4, and no
     ♣ K.Q.8.4   sane person breaks Rule 4. You should pass.

The Jump Overbid

The Jump Overbid is a strength-showing bid, and denotes a hand
that is too good for a simple overbid. It promises either:

(1) A good six-card suit with 7½–8 Playing Tricks or
(2) A hand containing two suits of at least five cards each.

It is important that the suits be self-supporting. The following
are proper overbids of 2 ♠ over an opposing 1 ◇:

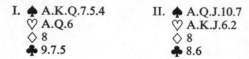

I. ♠ A.K.Q.7.5.4   II. ♠ A.Q.J.10.7
    ♡ A.Q.6   ♡ A.K.J.6.2
    ◇ 8   ◇ 8
    ♣ 9.7.5   ♣ 8.6

The jump overbid is a more satisfactory method of treating
these hands than the Informatory Double, because it gives specific
information about the bidder's hand, instead of asking for information from partner. Besides, they are not hands on which one
would wish partner to pass the Double for penalties.

Overbid in the Opponents' Suit

This call, forcing to Game, is a specialized form of Informatory
Double. You may have a hand so strong that you cannot afford to

allow the bidding to stop short of Game, but at the same time you wish for time to explore the possibilities. The immediate overcall in the opponents' suit by creating a forcing situation allows the bidding to proceed slowly, just as if you had opened the bidding with a Two Club bid. The bid often announces first-round control of the opposing suit, but this is not obligatory. Let us take the following hand:

W	E
♠ A.K.Q.6.5.3	♠ 7
♡ A.K.J.10.6	♡ Q.8.4.3
◇ 5	◇ 9.3.2
♣ A	♣ J.7.6.4.2

South opens 1 ◇, and West overbids 2 ◇. This enables the partnership to reach the slam in Hearts. Without this forcing bid West would have to shut his eyes and bid 6 ♠, which fails against four Spades in one hand.

Protection

Protection is something that is used too much at duplicate, too little at rubber Bridge. The beginner is advised to leave this section alone until he has acquired a certain proficiency. Indeed, it is probably best for each one to work out his own salvation. For all that, it must be briefly touched upon.

Protection is the reopening of the bidding by one or other Defender when the opposing strength is found to be limited by their willingness to let the bidding die below the Game level.

There are two situations to be discussed, not exhaustively, but so that the logic behind the action can be seen.

1. After the bidding has gone 1 ♠ by West, No Bid by North, No Bid by East, what are you, South, to do? If you refer to page 82 you will see that there South holding ♠ J.6.5 ♡ A.K.10.8.2 ◇ K.8 ♣ Q.J.7 had to pass, because a bid of 2 ♡ was too dangerous. In view of this, now that East has by his pass advertised a bad hand, it is your duty to protect your partner's pass, by reopening the bidding if your own holding warrants it. Two problems confront you, (a) Whether to reopen, (b) How to reopen. Let us assume you hold the West hand in the example referred to:

♠ 4
♡ Q.J.9.6
◇ A.10.6.2
♣ K.8.6.3

You have only 10 Points, it is true, but you know that your partner has something. Assume that Opener has a good hand of 17–18 Points. Add the 3–4 Points indicated by his partner's pass. That leaves a minimum of 8 for your partner and he may have as many as 14–15. Clearly you must not let the opponents play in a 1 ♠ contract, so you decide to reopen. What are you to bid?

Your 4—4—4—1 is the ideal pattern for an Informatory Double, so you reopen with a Double. Of course, you have not 13 high-card Points, but partner knows that you are bidding on some of his assumed values. In response to your Double partner says 3 ♡, and Game is easily reached.

The second situation is when the bidding has gone:

E	S	W	N
1 ♡	No	2 ♡	No
No	?	—	—

You hold ♠ A.Q.7.5.3 ♡ 7.4 ◇ K.10.6 ♣ 9.6.3. You passed over 1 ♡, because you were not good enough to bid 1 ♠. But you are good enough *now* to bid 2 ♠! Again partner is marked with some Points, and there is another important point to notice. Since Opener's suit has been raised this means that you are at least unlikely to run up against a bad Spade break.

These are the only two situations that we will discuss. Even these require very delicate handling. You must be sure that your partner is good enough to recognize what you are doing. You must also be sure that your opponents are good enough not to have hopelessly underbid. If you reopen and allow them to bid and make a Game, your partner will no longer regard you as one of the Top Ten.

Tricky as this protection is, it cannot be ignored. Failure to employ it results in a big loss over the year.

Quiz on Chapter 15

Right-hand opponent opens 1 ♠. What do you bid holding

(a)	♠ 7	♡ A.K.Q.9.6.4.2	◇ A.J.10	♣ 4.3
(b)	♠ —	♡ A.K.J.7.6	◇ A.Q.9.7	♣ K.Q.6.4
(c)	♠ Q.10.3	♡ A.10	◇ K.Q.8.7	♣ K.J.6.4
(d)	♠ —	♡ A.10.6.3	◇ K.10.8.2	♣ K.9.8.6.2
(e)	♠ 4	♡ 8.5	◇ K.Q.J.10.8.4.3.2	♣ 7.5

16

Defensive Responses

YOUR left-hand opponent has opened the bidding and your partner has overbid, right-hand opponent passes and now it is up to you. Your course of action is governed not only by your own holding, but by the strength shown by partner's bid.

1. Response to Minimum Overbid

Let us suppose that West opens 1 ♡, North says 1 ♠ and East passes. Your partner's bid promises four to five Playing Tricks and 9 Points upwards. Look at the negative side of the picture. He has not made a jump overbid and he has not doubled, so that quite a lot is needed from you for Game.

Raise his suit once with adequate trump support and about four Playing Tricks

e.g. ♠ K.9.7   ♡ 7.6   ◇ A.8.5.4   ♣ Q.J.6.2   11 Points.[1]

Give a double raise with good trump support and about five Playing Tricks

e.g. ♠ K.9.7.3   ♡ 7.6   ◇ A.8.5.4   ♣ K.Q.6   13 Points.

Raise to Game (distributional) with five-card trump support

e.g. ♠ K.9.7.5.3   ♡ 7   ◇ A.9.8.5.4   ♣ Q.6   13 Points.

Raise to Game (balanced) with good trump support and 16 high-card Points

e.g. ♠ K.9.7.3   ♡ 7.6   ◇ A.Q.4   ♣ A.Q.J.6   17 Points.

Take out in a new suit. This must be constructive and not founded on fear.

e.g. bid 2 ◇ on ♠ 7.3   ♡ 7.6   ◇ A.Q.J.9.5   ♣ A.8.7.5   11 Points.

No Trumps Responses. These operate as if partner had opened the bidding but they are stronger, e.g. 1 NT 11–12 Points, 2 NT 13–14 Points, 3 NT 16–17 Points, with a stop in the Opener's suit.

Forcing Take-outs. These operate as normally but must be stronger.

[1] Distributional for raising partner's suit.

Bid in opponents' suit. This is forcing to Game and shows void or singleton in the opposing suit with 16 high-card Points—a hand too good for a direct raise to Game, 19–21 Points.

2. Response to Pre-emptive Overbid

Almost always you should pass. But it is possible to raise or take out constructively. Let us assume that the bidding has gone West 1 ◇, North 4 ♡, East No Bid. Your partner is only promising seven or eight Playing Tricks according to vulnerability. So you see that you require three very Quick Tricks, including at least two Aces, to raise to 6 ♡. Holding ♠ A.8.7.4 ♡ K.6.4 ◇ 5 ♣ A.K.9.8.3 you would be justified in putting partner to 6 ♡, but you need the two first-round and one second-round controls. As I have said, it is possible to have a constructive take-out, but it is very difficult to convince partner of it! If, after the same bidding 1 ◇, 4 ♡, No Bid, you held the ten top Spades and bid 4 ♠, partner would surely take you out into 5 ♡, on the assumption that your Spade bid was a cue bid. That brings us back to the opening remark—you should almost always pass.

3. Response to No Trumps Overbid

These are the same as if partner had opened the bidding.

4. Response to Jump Overbid

West bids 1 ◇, North 2 ♠, East No Bid.

Partner has announced 7½–8 Playing Tricks and a self-supporting suit, so you can

Raise once with two small trumps, one certain and one possible Trick

e.g. ♠ 6.4 ♡ A.8.6.2 ◇ 7.5.4 ♣ K.J.9.5 8 Points.

Raise to Game with two small trumps, two certain and one possible Trick

e.g. ♠ 6.4 ♡ A.8.6.2 ◇ 7.5.4 ♣ A.Q.9.5 10 Points.

5. Response to Informatory Double

The partner of the defender who doubles for a take-out is bound to make a positive bid, unless the intervention of the right-hand opponent relieves him of this obligation (for exception see below).

If your partner doubles informatorily he is asking two things:

1. Your long suit.
2. Your overall strength.

First of all, you must be quite clear what is the minimum holding which can be considered good in these circumstances. Your partner, with 13 high-card Points *plus* his singleton (or void) in the opposing suit, has at least 16 distributional Points for you. Therefore if you have 10–11 Points you have enough for Game. Even 7–8 may be enough if partner has a maximum.

Let us assume that West bids 1 ♡, North doubles and East passes.

With 0–8 Points make the minimum bid in your longest suit.

e.g. ♠ Q.7.4.3 ♡ 8.7.4 ◇ J.6.4 ♣ Q.4.3 bid 1 ♠
or ♠ A.J.9.6.3 ♡ 7.4 ◇ 7.6.4 ♣ Q.4.3 bid 1 ♠

With 9 or more Points make a jump take-out in your longest suit.

e.g. ♠ A.J.9.6.3 ♡ 7.6.4 ◇ J.4 ♣ K.4.3 bid 2 ♠

You may make this jump bid in a four-card suit provided the Response is not above the two level. (With a fair hand prefer four-card Major to five-card Minor.)

e.g. ♠ K.J.9.3 ♡ 7.6.4 ◇ 7.6 ♣ A.Q.4.3

With a six-card Major suit make a jump take-out on 7–8 Points.

e.g. ♠ A.9.7.6.5.3 ♡ 7.6 ◇ K.6.4 ♣ 4.3

With a very bad hand it is the duty of the Responder to avert any disaster, by using intelligence. For example, if you hold

♠ 8.7.5.3 ♡ 7.5.4 ◇ Q.7.4.2 ♣ 8.6

bid 1 ♠ instead of 2 ◇, as the bidding is kept lower.

Sometime you may be confronted with the following nightmare:

♠ 8.7.5 ♡ 9.6.5.3 ◇ 10.7.2 ♣ 9.7.6

Your only four-card suit is the opponents'. What are you to do? Make the cheapest bid—1 ♠. DO NOT bid 1 NT.

No Trumps Responses

1 NT promises a guard in the opposing suit and 4–9 Points

e.g. ♠ 10.6.5 ♡ K.J.7.5 ◇ Q.6.4.3 ♣ J.5

But prefer a Response in a four-card Major, and bid 1 ♠ with

e.g. ♠ Q.9.7.6 ♡ K.J.7.5 ◇ 10.6.5 ♣ J.5

2 NT promises a guard in the opposing suit and 10 Points.

e.g. ♠ 10.6.5 ♡ K.J.7.5 ◇ Q.6.4.3 ♣ A.5

The Pass

This is not a bid made on a worthless hand. It is a calculated decision that (a) the opposing bid will be defeated, (b) there is little future elsewhere. To pass partner's Double you require five almost solid trumps. You are prepared for and want a trump lead by partner.

With ♠ 7.4 ♡ K.Q.J.9.8 ◊ K.7.5 ♣ 10.5.2 it is correct to pass.

With ♠ 7.4 ♡ K.7.6.4.2 ◊ K.7.5 ♣ 10.5.2 it is incorrect. There is no certainty of defeating the opposing bid. You should bid 1 NT.

Free Response

If right-hand opponent bids you are released from your obligation to reply if your hand is worthless. But you may bid a five-card Major at the one level or a six-card Major at the two level with as little as 3–4 Points.

Let us assume the bidding has gone West 1 ♣, North Double, East 1 ◊. You may bid 1 ♠ on

♠ Q.9.8.5.4   ♡ Q.6.4   ◊ 9.8.3   ♣ 6.5

Again, after 1 ♣, Double, 2 ♣, you may bid 2 ♠ with

♠ K.8.7.5.4.2   ♡ J.7.3   ◊ 8.6   ♣ 9.3

If the right-hand opponent re-doubles do not rescue partner on a very weak hand, but bid any five-card suit at the one or even two level. This saves him from having to bid a four-card suit for which you have no support. With no five-card suit and a trickless hand let partner do his own rescuing.

6. Response to Bid in Opponents' Suit

As this is nothing but an Informatory Double on a grand scale, you should make the same Responses that you would make if partner had doubled. The only difference is that you must carry on until Game is reached, or the opponents have been subjected to a Penalty Double.

7. Response to Protective Reopening

When right-hand opponent's one bid is passed up to your partner.

e.g. East 1 ♠, South No Bid, West No Bid, North? (see page 86). Your action depends upon *how* North reopens. You simply add your Points to his advertised minimum and proceed accordingly.

If he doubles give him a minimum of 10–11 high-card Points.

If he bids 1 NT give him 9–10 balanced Points.

If he makes a simple overbid give him a five-card suit and not more than 10 Points.

If he makes a Jump bid give him a five-card suit and the strength of a Double.

Reflections on Defensive Bidding

On page 83 it was said that for a Double to be informatory the opposing bid must be in a suit. That means that, if your right-hand opponent bids 1 NT, a Double by you is for penalties. In other words you must have the Contract beaten in your own hand. This is only logical. If the opposing bid is a strong NT, it is most unlikely that you or the opponents can have a Game, so that a part-score is all that is at stake. If you double informatorily and find the remaining few points with your partner, you may well fine the opponents 300 or 500 Points. If, however, your left-hand opponent has the balance and re-doubles, the take-out your partner is forced to make may go down 700.

Thus the Double of a strong NT, either immediately or as a re-opening, is a gamble for a top or a bottom.

Against the weak NT, the Informatory Double has more justification, for it is possible for you to be missing a Game, and the carnage, if partner has the Points to leave in the Double, can be quite something. Against that, if the left-hand opponent has the Points, there are even more cards that can be 'over you'.

Quiz on Chapter 16

1. West bids 1 ♡, North says 1 ♠, East passes. What do you say holding

    ♠ 8.5   ♡ K.8.7   ♢ A.J.6.4   ♣ K.Q.8.6

2. West bids 1 ♡, North says Double, East passes. What do you say holding

    ♠ J.7.6   ♡ K.10.8.2   ♢ A.5.3   ♣ Q.7.6

3. West bids 1 ♡, North says 1 ♠, East passes. What do you say holding

    ♠ 9   ♡ 8.7.4   ♢ A.J.6.5.2   ♣ K.6.5.3

4. West bids 1 ♠, North and East pass. What do you say holding

    ♠ 7.5   ♡ K.J.6.5   ♢ A.7.2   ♣ K.9.6.4

5. West bids 1 ♡, North doubles, East passes. What do you say holding

    ♠ K.J.9.3   ♡ 8.4.2   ♢ K   ♣ A.9.8.4.2

17

The Penalty Double

THE Penalty Double, as was said on page 17, challenges the Declarer's ability to meet his liabilities. In support of his challenge the doubler is prepared to increase both the premiums and penalties. Therefore the mathematical odds involved are an important factor. The opportunity to double an opposing Contract may occur in one of two bidding situations, either uncontested or competitive.

Doubles of Uncontested Bids

(a) *Slam Bid*. The Double of an uncontested slam bid has been rightly termed the Sucker's Double. Let us look at the mathematics of it. Assuming that your opponents are at least reasonable players, it is unlikely that they will go down more than a Trick. At a love score, if they go one down doubled, you score 100 instead of 50. If they make their doubled Contract, they score $500 + 360 + 50 = 910$, instead of 680 (Major suit). If they should re-double they score $500 + 720 + 50 = 1270$. Your anxiety to get an extra 50 has cost you 230 in the first case and 590 in the second.

There are other considerations. Even if you know that they cannot make the slam in the denomination bid, are you sure they cannot make it in another? Are you going to warn them something is wrong, and guide them into the right slam bid?

I remember many years ago hearing the dealer on my right open the bidding with a startling Seven Diamonds. I held nothing in my hand but Q.x.x in diamonds and passed. The Contract duly went one down. Seven Spades was on ice! Had I doubled, the declarer, so he told me, would have bid 7 ♠.

Again, by your Double you may give the Declarer the key to the play of the hand. He may be led to adopt an unnatural line of play by knowing the only card or cards you can have to justify the Double.

Is it ever right to double a slam? Yes, there are two occasions.

1. When you hold an Ace against a 7 NT bid, *and it is your lead*, or you hold A.K of Trumps against a small slam, *and there is no switch*.

2. When you want a specific lead from partner (see page 64).

(b) *Game Bid*. The same considerations largely apply here too.

You must be sure that there is no switch available, and that your Double will not show the Declarer how to play the hand. Here are two golden rules for such situations:

 1. *Never double if you expect to get Declarer only one down.*
 2. *Do not double without a trump trick.*

Doubles of Competitive Bids

(*a*) *At the Lower Levels.* The lower levels of competitive bidding, as was said at the beginning of Chapter 12, prove a great source of loss to the weak player. It is particularly his overbids at the two level that have kept the good player in smoked salmon and silk shirts for over a quarter of a century.

You should, therefore, be alert to double any intervening bid at the two level after partner has opened the bidding. The ideal requirements are:

1. Shortage in partner's suit. 2. Four (or five) trumps to an Honour. 3. Two Tricks outside. The hand given on page 82 meets all these requirements. e.g. after 1 ♠ from partner and 2 ♡ from right-hand opponent, you double with

♠ 4   ♡ Q.J.9.6   ◇ A.10.6.2   ♣ K.8.6.3

The shortage in partner's suit is most important. If you have some length in it you may be missing Game worth more than the Double, and you jeopardize your partner's defensive Tricks in his suit. For instance, after 1 ♠ overbid by 2 ♡, if you hold

♠ Q.10.6.5   ♡ A.Q.10.4   ◇ 7.5   ♣ K.7.3

do not double but raise to 4 ♠.

The two outside Tricks are also essential. If you double on trump length alone, the following disaster is likely to occur e.g. after 1 ♠ overbid by 2 ◇, if you double with

♠ 8.7.4   ♡ 9.3   ◇ K.J.9.6.5   ♣ 10.6.3

West now bids 2 ♡, which your partner doubles, and the Contract is easily made.

Overbids of two in a Minor suit may be doubled with even more freedom. If the Contract is made it does not give the opponents Game, and if the overbidder has 'spoken out of turn' the penalty may be large.

e.g. after 1 ♠ overbid by 2 ◇ you double holding:

♠ A.5   ♡ K.J.9.4   ◇ J.9.6.2   ♣ 9.6.4

In all these low-level Doubles partnership co-operation is essential. The Doubles are to a certain extent tentative, and partner is expected to take out any such Double with a hand that is unsuitable, either too good or too defensively weak.

e.g. ♠ K.Q.10.8.6.3 ♡ A.7.6 ◇ 5 ♣ 8.7.5 is clearly too weak, and ♠ K.Q.J.10.6.3 ♡ A.7.6 ◇ 5 ♣ A.J.5 is too strong.

The co-operative hand is ♠ K.J.9.4 ♡ A.10.6.3 ◇ 8.5 ♣ A.J.5, and with this you pass happily.

To leave in a Double when you are void in the suit is wrong. To say that your void 'leaves all the more for partner' is a fallacious argument.

(b) *At the Higher Levels*. Again, in Chapter 15, it was said that the higher levels of competitive bidding prove the greatest stumbling-block to the good player. A moment's reflection will show you that faulty judgment here can cost a tremendous number of Points in the year. Let us suppose that your side has bid up to Four Hearts and that the opponents now bid Four Spades.

You have to decide whether to bid 5 ♡ or to double 4 ♠. If you judge the position wrongly you are faced with varying degrees of loss.

e.g. you decide to double 4 ♠, and

1. Opponents make 4 ♠ doubled when you would have made 5 ♡—very serious.

2. Opponents make 4 ♠ doubled when you would have gone one down in 5 ♡—serious.

3. Opponents go one down when you would have made 5 ♡—serious.

Again, you decide to bid 5 ♡, and

1. You go one down when opponents would have gone three down—very serious.

2. You go one down when opponents would have gone one down—not serious.

The last situation is labelled 'not serious', but it is still a big source of loss if you judge wrongly every time. However, the good player cannot be expected to get the right answer without fail, and he prefers this 'not serious' loss as a form of insurance. You will notice that bidding one more is on the whole a less costly error. In competitive situations at the slam level, when the hands are clearly freakish, you should pay this insurance, if you have any doubt whatever about beating the opposing Contract.

Re-doubling

As a general rule do not re-double, until you have become at least a fair player. Apart from the really serious loss you may sustain if you run into a freak distribution of the cards, there is the added danger of driving the opponents back into their suit, and finding that the penalty they pay is negligible compared with the amount of your doubled Contract successfully fulfilled.

Sacrifice Bidding

Shrewd sacrificing pays, but wild flag-flying is to be deprecated. There is nothing more damaging to the morale than losing a big rubber. Pay a reasonable price to stop the opponents' game, *if you are sure they can make it*, provided that the score is either Love-all or Game-all. If you are vulnerable and opponents are not, it is better not to take a two-trick penalty—these have a habit of turning into three down. If you are Love and the opponents are Game, here is a golden rule—only stop the opposing Game at *bargain* prices, that is 100 or at the most 300. Do not forget, it is still three to one on their winning the rubber.

No Quiz on this chapter. Re-read Doubles of competitive bids at the Lower Levels.

18

The Declarer's Play

The sources of Tricks

TRICKS come from three sources:

1. Honour Cards.   2. Long Cards.   3. Ruffs.

The first two apply equally to No Trumps and trump Contracts, but the third belongs exclusively to trump Contracts. To understand 1. and 2. let us suppose that the Heart suit is divided between the four hands as follows:

J.9.5

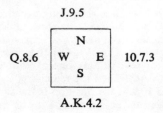

Q.8.6   W   E   10.7.3

A.K.4.2

South leads the Ace, to which West, North and East play the Six, Five and Three. South now leads the King, on which fall the Eight, Nine and Seven. South now leads the Two, which West wins with the Queen, the Knave and Ten falling. South is now left with the Four, which is automatically the ranking card, because there is no other card of that suit left unplayed. This is a long-card trick for South to make when he gets the lead again.

To understand 3. let us suppose that the last five cards of a deal are as follows:

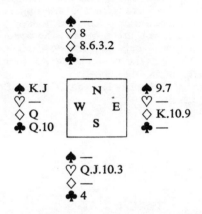

It is South's lead. If he plays out his trumps he will be left with the Club, which West will win. But if South first leads the Club he can ruff it in Dummy, and so lose no Tricks. If, on the other hand, North had the lead and led a Diamond for South to ruff before he played out his trumps, South would still be left with a losing Club. From this we can see that, in order to gain a Trick or Tricks, the ruff must be taken in the hand with the shorter trumps.

Development of Tricks at No Trumps

Development by Force

If you are dealt A.K.Q in a suit, you have three ready-developed Tricks, which you are at liberty to play, or 'cash', any time you have the lead. But life is not always so easy—you have to work for your Tricks. Suppose you have K.Q.J.10.9. The solidity of the suit makes it simple for you to play one of your cards, on which an opponent plays his Ace. Then the remaining four Tricks are yours. If your suit is Q.J.10.9.8, the position is the same, except that you have to lose the lead to the opposing King as well as the Ace.

Development by Finesse

In Chapter 2 you were told that, after the Leader has led to a Trick, the other three players must play in strict clockwise rotation. A little thought about this should show you that cards may have a positional advantage or disadvantage. For example, let us suppose that your partner leads a small card of a suit in which you hold A.Q. If your right-hand opponent holds the King and follows with a small card, you will be able to win the Trick with your Queen.

This attempt to win a Trick with a card not the highest in the suit is called a finesse. It is an attempt to exploit an assumed positional advantage. A finesse may be repeated. Suppose the Diamond suit is divided between you and Dummy as follows:

◇ 7.5.4.2

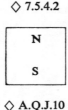

◇ A.Q.J.10

You play the Two from Dummy, and, assuming positional advantage (that East has the King), you finesse the Ten, after a small card from East. Now you get back into Dummy with a high card in another suit and you repeat the operation. In this way you make four Diamond Tricks, instead of three if you had employed development by force. Let us transpose the cards a little:

◇ Q.J.10.9

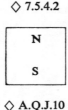

◇ A.5.4.2

The operation is basically the same. The Queen is led from Dummy, and if East does not play the King, the Queen wins. Dummy still has the lead and continues with the Knave, and again you win all four Tricks. Let us make another change:

D

◇ 10.9.4.2

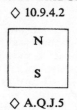

◇ A.Q.J.5

Dummy leads the Ten. If that wins the Trick he follows with a small card and finesses the Knave. If eight cards have now appeared, no further finesse is necessary, as the King must drop, but if East still has King and another, Dummy must be re-entered for a third finesse.

The last two positions, imperfectly understood, lead the beginner to embark on so-called finesses which can do him no good. For example:

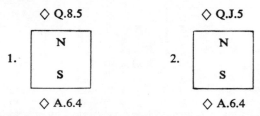

He leads the Queen in 1. with the mistaken idea that he is getting some advantage. But by leading the Queen he restricts himself to one Trick—the Ace—wherever the King may be. In order to win two Tricks he must now assume that West has the King. He plays first the Ace, then leads a small card from his hand up to the Queen in Dummy. If West has the King, the Queen must make either immediately or later.

In 2. the lead of the Queen is equally mistaken. The Declarer already has two Tricks by force, and cannot gain a third by this pseudo-finesse. It is the absence of the Ten in either hand that makes this play useless. It is correct if two Tricks only are needed *without losing the lead*.

The only way to win three Tricks in the suit is to play the Ace and hope that the King is singleton in one opposing hand.

From what was said about the absence of the Ten, you may formulate this rule:

It is useless to lead a card for a finesse, unless you hold as well the two cards in sequence immediately below it.

Development by Compound Finesse

With different combinations of honours it is possible to finesse against more than one card in the opponents' hands.

It will perhaps be helpful to go back to our basic position:

◇ A.Q

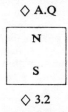

◇ 3.2

We saw that with this position we can win two Tricks, by leading from the South hand, only if West holds the King. But let us extend this position to the following:

◇ A.Q.10

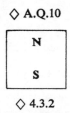

◇ 4.3.2

Here we can win two Tricks, by leading from the South hand and playing the Ten from Dummy, if West holds *either* King *or* Knave. Furthermore, if West holds both of these honours, we shall win all three Tricks by this manœuvre. We were able to 'surround' the opposing King (Rank 2) because we held the cards either side of it, that is Ace and Queen (Ranks 1 and 3). Similarly we surrounded the opposing Knave (Rank 4) with our Queen and Ten (Ranks 3 and 5).

Now let us examine another position:

◇ A.J.10

◇ 4.3.2

Here we hold Ranks 1, 4 and 5, while our opponents hold Ranks 2 and 3. The fact that their Ranks are sequential makes it impossible for us to surround completely. Either the King or the Queen must make a Trick. But we can take advantage of position and win two Tricks, if West holds either both or one of the honours, by leading from South and playing Dummy's Ten.

There are many other combinations, which we cannot deal with here, but they are all variations on the same theme. By the way, it might be as well to point out that though we have illustrated the finesse with honour cards, because that is the commonest form in which it appears, a finesse against a 'spot' card does not differ, e.g.

◇ 9.7

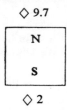

◇ 2

Here we lead the Two and finesse the Seven, against West's presumed (or proved) Eight.

A word of warning must be injected here. The novice, seeing that a finesse is a method of getting something for nothing, is blind to the dangers that it may bring. This you will learn later.

A beginner looks for any finesse he can make, but an expert sees how he can avoid it.

Development by Ducking

Ducking is an entry-preserving play. To duck is to play a low card, so that, by the immediate concession of a loser or losers, the high card or cards may be preserved as entries to bring in the rest of the suit. There are two types of the duck:

1. The Obligatory Duck

Suppose that the Clubs are divided between you and Dummy thus,

♣ A.K.6.5.4

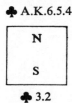

♣ 3.2

and that it is essential to make 4 Tricks in the suit for your Contract. The opponents hold between them Q.J.10.9.8.7, and we must assume the most favourable division of three in each hand, otherwise our task is hopeless. If we lead the ♣ 2 and win with the Ace, win a second Trick with the King, and then lead a third round, it is clear that the opponents will now be exhausted of the suit, and that the two small cards in Dummy are now established as long-card Tricks. But they are frozen assets, because there is no entry to Dummy to cash them. The remedy is simple. On the lead of the ♣ 2 we play, not the Ace or King, but the Four, allowing one or other of our opponents to win the Trick. When we regain the lead in the South hand we play the ♣ 3, and the Ace and King will drop the two Clubs that are held by each opponent. Now, with the lead still in Dummy, we can make the two established Tricks.

2. The Safety Duck

This time the Club suit is divided thus,

♣ A.K.Q.5.4

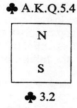

♣ 3.2

and we need only four Tricks from the suit. Again, there are six cards against us, but we do not have to assume the most favourable 3—3 division. As a matter of fact, the odds are six to four in favour of a 4—2 split. We can afford the luxury of a safety duck, to ensure four Tricks if the suit breaks 4—2. If it turns out that the suit was divided 3—3, we have lost a Trick, but that is a small insurance.

A duck and a finesse may be combined in development:

♡ A.Q.6.5.4

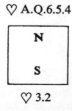

♡ 3.2

Here we have to assume the 3—3 break and the King with West. We duck the first round and finesse the Queen on the second. The odds are well against this effort succeeding, and if your Contracts are depending on such plays, it is time that your bidding was tightened up!

Development by Unblocking

Suppose the Spades are divided thus:

♠ A.J.5.4.3

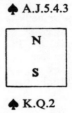

♠ K.Q.2

If you play Dummy's Ace first, you have blocked the suit, and though you can make your King and Queen, you cannot make the long cards. Two Tricks are lost. If you play the King and Queen from your own hand first, you can make all five Tricks. Elementary as this example may be, it is essential to understand that unblocking on certain hands is vital to the fulfilment of the Contract, e.g.

1. Singleton Unblock.

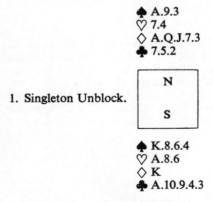

   ♠ A.9.3
   ♡ 7.4
   ◇ A.Q.J.7.3
   ♣ 7.5.2

   ♠ K.8.6.4
   ♡ A.8.6
   ◇ K
   ♣ A.10.9.4.3

You are trying to make 3 NT against the opening lead of the ♡ K. After winning the first Trick you must play the ◇ K, to unblock the suit. This allows you to make five Diamonds, two Spades, a Heart and a Club for your nine Tricks.

Here is another example:

♠ 7.6.4
♡ A.8
◇ K.Q.10.9.7
♣ 9.6.5

2. Singleton Overtake.

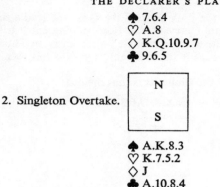

♠ A.K.8.3
♡ K.7.5.2
◇ J
♣ A.10.8.4

Once more you play 3 NT, against the lead of the ♡ Q. You win the first Trick with the King in your own hand, and immediately play the ◇ J and overtake it in Dummy. You lead Diamonds until the Ace is forced out. Now you can get back into Dummy with the ♡ A and make the remaining Diamonds. Suppose that you had not overtaken the ◇ J. The opponent with the Ace would not have played it. Now you could have used the ♡ A to establish the Diamonds, but you would have had no entry to enable you to make them.

Here is another instructive example:

♠ 8.4
♡ Q.J.10
◇ K.Q.J.9.3.2
♣ 8.6

3. Unblock to post-pone entry.

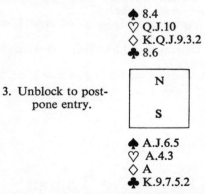

♠ A.J.6.5
♡ A.4.3
◇ A
♣ K.9.7.5.2

West leads the ♡ 5 against your 3 NT. On Dummy's Ten East follows with the Six. It is your Trick already. But if you do not unblock by overtaking with the Ace you will not be able to get into Dummy to cash those lovely Diamonds. The correct procedure

is to win Trick 1 with the ♡ A, play off the ♢ A, and lead a small
Heart. Now West cannot prevent you from gaining entry to the
Dummy. You have, in effect, postponed your entry in Dummy
till later, when you are ready to use it, after the ♢ A has been un-
blocked.

Let us assume that the Club suit is thus divided:

♣ A.K.Q.6.2

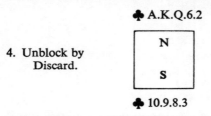

4. Unblock by
    Discard.

♣ 10.9.8.3

You need all five Tricks for Contract. Only if one opponent holds
four Clubs can you be beaten. So you play to the Ace in Dummy,
and both opponents follow. You smile happily—the Game is in
sight. But not if you played the ♣ 3 on the Ace, King or Queen.
In that case you will find the nasty Ten stopping you from making
the fifth Club. (It is assumed that one opponent held J.x.x, so that
you were not given an opportunity to recover from your mistake.)

Quiz on Chapter 18

1. What are the three sources of Tricks?
2. How do you define a simple finesse?
3. With Q.8.5 in Dummy and A.6.4 in your own hand, how do
you play to make two Tricks?
4. With A.K.6.5.4 in Dummy and 3.2 in your own hand, how
do you play to make four Tricks?
5. With A.K.Q.10.9 in Dummy and 3.2 in your own hand, how
do you play to ensure four Tricks?

19

Declarer's Play at No Trumps

WHEN Dummy goes down after the opening lead, the Declarer's
first task is to study the combined assets of the two hands, and to
plan his play. Let us suppose that you opened 1 NT on the South

hand and were raised to 3 NT. Now you have to make your nine Tricks after the lead of the ♣ K.

♠ A.8.4
♡ 9.7.3
◇ A.Q.6.5.2
♣ 8.4

┌─────────┐
│   N   │
│   │
│   S   │
└─────────┘

♠ K.Q.6
♡ A.Q.J
◇ J.10.9.4
♣ A.5.3

Step One

Count up your established winners.

These are three Spades, one Heart, one Diamond, one Club— six Tricks in all, three short of your Contract.

Step Two

Count up establishable winners.

As you have properly assimilated the previous chapter, you will readily see that the Diamond suit can be developed by finesse. If the King is with West, you can develop four more Tricks, if it is with East three more. In the Hearts suit, too, you see that with the King in East's hand you can make two more Tricks by finesse. Thus with visions of making twelve Tricks, you win the first Trick with the ♣ Ace, and lead the ◇ J. East wins with the King and returns a Club for West to take four more Tricks. You are one down, and partner asks you if you do not really prefer Canasta. What went wrong? You entirely overlooked:

Step Three

Count the opponents' potential winners. Which are inescapable? Which are avoidable?

How should you have played the hand? You should have studied the card led, and decided that West had probably opened his long suit (see Defensive Play), headed by a sequence (see Opening Leads). You should have assumed that he had five or even six cards in the suit.

Let us now follow the train of reasoning that an expert employs. 'I have six ready-made winners, and I can develop three or more in Diamonds. West may have four winners in Clubs, after my Ace is forced out, but if he has five Clubs, then East has only three. So if I do not play my Ace until the third round of the suit, East will be unable to return a Club, on winning the Diamond finesse, if he holds the King.'

Now you see that you ought to have played your ♣ Ace, not at Trick 1, but at Trick 3. By doing this you are using one of the Declarer's greatest weapons, especially at No Trumps play, the HOLD UP. At first sight it appears to be a simple ducking play, but it is really a counter-duck. You force the opponents to take their Tricks when it is disadvantageous for them to do so.

After East wins with the ◇ K, he returns a Heart. This finesse you refuse, as you have your nine Tricks in sight, and the first consideration is to MAKE YOUR CONTRACT. At this point you say: Suppose East had another Club. What would happen? If East had four Clubs, then West would have only four Clubs. The opponents could take the ◇ K and three Clubs, still leaving nine tricks for you.

Governing the play of every hand is the Time Factor. The play of a 3 NT hand is a race, in which the Declarer is trying to establish and make nine Tricks before the opponents can make five. Normally, the Declarer seeks to establish his longest suit, as there are more tricks to be found there, but reference to the Time Factor may show that certain Tricks cannot be established quickly enough. Let us examine this 3 NT hand:

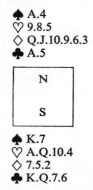

♠ A.4
♡ 9.8.5
◇ Q.J.10.9.6.3
♣ A.5

```
┌─────────┐
│    N    │
│         │
│    S    │
└─────────┘
```

♠ K.7
♡ A.Q.10.4
◇ 7.5.2
♣ K.Q.7.6

West leads the ♠ Q. What are your prospects? You have established two Spades, one Heart and three Clubs. Three more

Tricks are wanted. The Diamond suit will clearly provide four more. But there are two controls, or 'stoppers', to force out. Now stoppers have not only Trick value but lead value, and every lead is a unit of time, or a tempo, as it is called in Chess. Your opponents hold two tempos in your suit, and you hold two tempos in theirs, but as the rules provide that the player on the left of the Declarer has the opening lead, the opponents have thereby an extra tempo. This means that they will win the establishment race. So, if you attempt to develop Diamonds, you must go down. The only other hope is the Heart suit. You must play for the double finesse, that is, assume that East has both the King and the Knave. This is the only play for the Contract. You win Trick 1 with the ♠ Ace, lead the ♡ 9 and let it run if not covered. The double finesse is right, and you make your Contract. The Time Factor showed you that the Diamond suit must be abandoned in favour of a play that, though speculative, has at least a chance of success.

Another Look at the Hold Up

Let us study the following two hands:

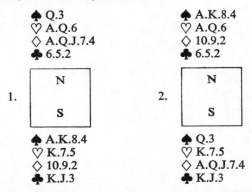

1.
♠ Q.3
♡ A.Q.6
◇ A.Q.J.7.4
♣ 6.5.2

2.
♠ A.K.8.4
♡ A.Q.6
◇ 10.9.2
♣ 6.5.2

1.
♠ A.K.8.4
♡ K.7.5
◇ 10.9.2
♣ K.J.3

2.
♠ Q.3
♡ K.7.5
◇ A.Q.J.7.4
♣ K.J.3

In each the Contract is 3 NT, and the lead is the ♣ 7. East plays the ♣ Q. Despite the similarity between the two hands, the play diverges sharply at Trick 1.

In 1. the beginner is tempted to win the ♣ Q with the King, as he has a chance of making two Tricks in the suit, but a moment's reflection should show you the folly of such a move. Be obedient to the rules. Count up your Tricks. You have three Spades, three Hearts, one Diamond and a Club (if you want it) at once. The Diamond suit is the only hope for more. To develop it, and this is the important point, you have to finesse into the East hand. If you had held A.x.x in Clubs you would have used the hold-up play to exhaust East of Clubs. Then curb your greed and do the same with K.J.x. Once the Queen has been played the King and Knave become equals and are not subject to finesse.

In 2. the situation is quite different, as the Diamond finesse is taken into the West hand. Here it is right to win the first Trick, and the hold up would be insane, as it would endanger the Contract which is otherwise impregnable.

From these hands you should learn that, according to the position of the cards, one or other of your opponents becomes the dangerous hand—that is, the one that must be kept out of the lead.

The Hold Up with Two Stoppers

Sometimes, even when you have two controls in the opposing suit, it is essential to hold up. The following hand is worth serious study. If you can grasp why the hold up must be made on Trick 1, and not on Trick 3, you are starting to understand the play of the Dummy.

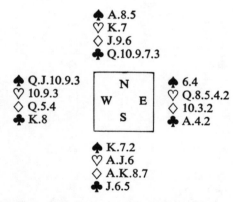

♠ A.8.5
♡ K.7
◇ J.9.6
♣ Q.10.9.7.3

♠ Q.J.10.9.3   ♠ 6.4
♡ 10.9.3   N   ♡ Q.8.5.4.2
◇ Q.5.4   W   E   ◇ 10.3.2
♣ K.8   S   ♣ A.4.2

♠ K.7.2
♡ A.J.6
◇ A.K.8.7
♣ J.6.5

Against your 3 NT, West leads the ♠ Q. Resources are six top Tricks, with three more to come from the Club suit.

You let West's Queen hold, and win Trick 2 with your King. You play a Club and East wins, but he has no Spade to return. Your hold up has deprived him of his lead value. Now you can knock out West's stopper while you still control his suit.

Knocking out the Dangerous Entry First

Here is one more important principle for you to understand and put into practice. You are playing 3 NT, and West leads the ♠ Q.

♠ 8.3
♡ 7.6.4.2
♢ A.J.9.4
♣ Q.7.5

```
┌─────────────┐
│      N      │
│             │
│      S      │
└─────────────┘
```

♠ A.K.7
♡ K.Q.J
♢ Q.10.7.6
♣ A.K.2

This time there is no need to hold up on Trick 1. I hope you now see why. You win with your King, and lead at once a Heart to extract West's fang, the Ace, if he should hold it. If West wins and leads another Spade, this time you do hold up. If West started with five Spades, East will have three and must be exhausted of them before you try the Diamond finesse.

Quiz on Chapter 19

1. What are the three steps to take before playing a card as Declarer?

2. What is the object of the Hold Up?

3. In each of the following 3 NT hands West leads a small Heart and East plays the Queen. Do you, or do you not, hold up?

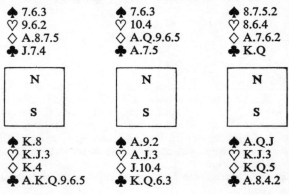

♠ 7.6.3   ♠ 7.6.3   ♠ 8.7.5.2
♡ 9.6.2   ♡ 10.4   ♡ 8.6.4
♢ A.8.7.5   ♢ A.Q.9.6.5   ♢ A.7.6.2
♣ J.7.4   ♣ A.7.5   ♣ K.Q

```
┌────────┐   ┌────────┐   ┌────────┐
│   N    │   │   N    │   │   N    │
│        │   │        │   │        │
│   S    │   │   S    │   │   S    │
└────────┘   └────────┘   └────────┘
```

♠ K.8   ♠ A.9.2   ♠ A.Q.J
♡ K.J.3   ♡ A.J.3   ♡ K.J.3
♢ K.4   ♢ J.10.4   ♢ K.Q.5
♣ A.K.Q.9.6.5   ♣ K.Q.6.3   ♣ A.8.4.2

20

Declarer's Play with a Trump Suit

EVERY play that is available to the Declarer at No Trumps is also available when there are trumps, but the power of the trump suit directs the entire course of the hand. With a trump suit there are three new factors:

1. Ruffing Tricks in the short hand.
2. Ruffing Stoppers.
3. Ruffing Entries.

Examine the following hand, and see the tremendous power of the trump element.

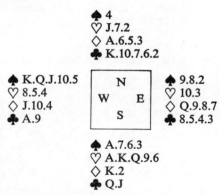

```
                    ♠ 4
                    ♡ J.7.2
                    ◇ A.6.5.3
                    ♣ K.10.7.6.2
  ♠ K.Q.J.10.5    ┌──────────┐    ♠ 9.8.2
  ♡ 8.5.4         │    N     │    ♡ 10.3
  ◇ J.10.4        │  W   E   │    ◇ Q.9.8.7
  ♣ A.9           │    S     │    ♣ 8.5.4.3
                  └──────────┘
                    ♠ A.7.6.3
                    ♡ A.K.Q.9.6
                    ◇ K.2
                    ♣ Q.J
```

In No Trumps South has eight top Tricks, and four more can be set up in Clubs. But he cannot fulfil a Contract of 3 NT, because West must make four Spades and the Ace of Clubs. But he will fulfil a Contract of 6 ♡ easily. He wins the opening Spade lead, plays two rounds of Hearts, ending in Dummy, and leads a small Club to the Queen. West wins, but cannot make another trick. There are two points to notice here:

1. The single trump in Dummy is sufficient to stop the run of the Spade suit.

2. Dummy has ruffing Tricks, for two Spades can be trumped in

Dummy, but the Declarer does not need them, as the Club suit supplies enough discards.

Let us make a slight change in the hands, by giving Dummy South's three small Spades in return for three small Clubs, as follows:

♠ 7.6.4.3
♡ J.7.2
◇ A.6.5.3
♣ K.10

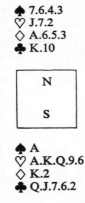

♠ A
♡ A.K.Q.9.6
◇ K.2
♣ Q.J.7.6.2

This time South, after winning the Spade lead, draws three rounds of trumps before he plays a Club. There is no need to keep a trump in Dummy, because there is no job for it to do. The ruffing stopper is provided by South. This illustrates that most expressive term that Culbertson used of a 'busy' trump. In the original hand Dummy's one trump was busy, but in the rearranged hand they were all idle.

Once you understand this question of busy and idle trumps you are well on the way to mastering trump management. You can divide all hands into three classes:

1. Where trump drawing is immediate.
2. Where trump drawing is postponed.
3. Where trump drawing is abandoned.

In class 1 we include hands like the last one, where there is no ruffing to be done, and play proceeds exactly as in a No Trumps hand. The beginner finds these easy.

In class 2 we group a large percentage of suit Contracts. These require careful handling, and often split-second timing. The reasons for postponement or partial postponement are various. We can examine some instances:

	A.		**B.**

♠ J.9.5.4
♡ A.K.Q
♢ 8.7.4
♣ Q.J.5

♠ Q.9.4
♡ 7.5.2
♢ A.K.8.6.5
♣ 9.7

```
        N
  A.
        S
```

```
        N
  B.
        S
```

♠ K.Q.10.7.6
♡ 8.5
♢ A.9.3
♣ K.6.2

♠ A.K.10.7.3
♡ 9.6.4
♢ 9.2
♣ A.8.5

♠ 7.6.2
♡ 8.7
♢ A.K.9.5
♣ K.9.8.2

♠ Q.10.5
♡ 6.5.2
♢ K.Q.10.9
♣ K.9.6

```
        N
  C.
        S
```

```
        N
  D.
        S
```

♠ A.K.Q.9.5
♡ K.Q.4
♢ 8.6
♣ Q.4.3

♠ A.K.J.8
♡ A.8.3
♢ J.6
♣ A.8.5.3

The contract in every case is 4 ♠.

In A West leads the ♢ K. South sees that, if he tries to draw trumps, he must lose the lead to the Ace. This will expose him to the loss of two Diamonds and a Club, or four Tricks in all, so that he will be one down. But, by playing first out Dummy's three Hearts, South can discard one of his losing Diamonds, and make his Contract. This illustrates *postponement of trump drawing to discard losers*.

In B the opponents cash three Heart Tricks, and then lead a Club. South's only hope of making his Contract is that the opponents have three Diamonds each. If they have, he can play ♢ A and ♢ K and ruff the third round, which will leave two established Tricks in Dummy. But to make them he needs an entry, and the trump Queen is the only possibility. So trumps cannot be drawn completely. South wins Trick 4 with the ♣ A, and then plays ♠ A and ♠ K. Both opponents follow, so that one trump is left outstanding. Now Ace, King and another Diamond, which is ruffed by South. As opponents followed three times, the last two Diamonds are good. South leads a trump to Dummy's Queen. This executes two operations—it draws the last enemy trump, and it gives the vital entry to make the set-up Diamonds. This illustrates *postponement of trump drawing to preserve entry for set-up suit*.

In C West leads a small Diamond, which Dummy's King wins. If South draws the trumps, he will have two possible Heart losers, and two almost certain Club losers. His first lead from Dummy will therefore be a Heart to his King. West wins and returns another Diamond, won on the table. Another Heart to the Queen is followed by the third Heart, ruffed by Dummy. Now the trumps are drawn, and South can afford to lose two Club Tricks. He makes five trumps, two Diamonds, one Heart, and one Club. These nine Tricks together with the Heart ruff in Dummy gives him the required ten Tricks. This illustrates *postponement of trump drawing to ruff losers*.

In D West leads the ♡ K, won with South's Ace. Declarer now plays two rounds of trumps, leaving the Ten in Dummy, and the ♢ Ace is forced out. Opponents make two Heart Tricks. If a fourth round of Hearts is led, Dummy can trump it. Had South drawn trumps, he would have found four trumps in one opposing hand impossible to cope with. If he drew four rounds of trumps, he would have no trump left to stop the run of the Hearts. If he drew three rounds, in order to ruff a Heart, he would leave the opponent with an established trump—enough to break the Contract. This illustrates *postponement of trump drawing to avoid forcing the long hand*.

In class 3 we place the cross ruff. Here trumps are never drawn, but Declarer and Dummy make their trumps separately. Let us take a typical hand:

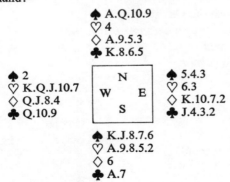

```
              ♠ A.Q.10.9
              ♡ 4
              ♢ A.9.5.3
              ♣ K.8.6.5
♠ 2                            ♠ 5.4.3
♡ K.Q.J.10.7      N            ♡ 6.3
♢ Q.J.8.4      W     E         ♢ K.10.7.2
♣ Q.10.9          S            ♣ J.4.3.2
              ♠ K.J.8.7.6
              ♡ A.9.8.5.2
              ♢ 6
              ♣ A.7
```

South is in a Contract of 7 ♠, and West leads the K ♡. South at once sees that the cross ruff is the correct play. He can make three Aces and a King in high cards, four Heart ruffs in Dummy, and three Diamond and two Club ruffs in his own hand. This gives thirteen tricks. As he has all the high trumps South is never in any danger of an over-ruff. He wins Trick 1 with ♡ A, and then cashes the ♣ A and ♣ K. This brings out a most important principle: *In a cross ruff, when two suits are being ruffed, the high cards in the third suit must be played early, to avoid an enemy ruff.*

If South failed to cash the Clubs early, he would allow East to discard Clubs on the third, fourth and fifth round of Hearts.

Quiz on Chapter 20

1. Give three reasons for postponing the drawing of trumps.

2. What precaution must you take when embarking on a cross ruff?

3.

♠ J.8.4	
♡ 7.3	
◇ A.8.6.2	
♣ K.Q.6.5	

N
S

South is playing 4 ♠. West leads a Diamond won with Dummy's Ace. What should be played to Trick 2?

♠ A.K.Q.7.6
♡ A.Q.4
◇ K.9
♣ 8.7.4

Table of Opening Leads

LEADING PARTNER'S SUIT

You hold	*You lead at NT*	*You lead at suit*
A.x.x.x	Lowest	A
A.x.x	Lowest	A
K.x.x or Q.x.x	Lowest	Lowest
K.Q.x	K	K
Q.J.x	Q	Q
x.x.x.x	Lowest	Lowest
x.x.x	Highest	Highest

This table is by no means comprehensive, and, it must be clearly realized, indicates the card to be led, if such a combination is chosen, and not the rightness of the choice.

21

Play of the Defenders

DEFENCE is unquestionably the hardest phase of Contract Bridge, for over and above the mere mechanics of leads and plays the demand is for concentration, for unremitting alertness and vigilance, for counting and deduction. In fact to be a good Defender is hard work, and those who are mentally lazy are not going to be proficient in this department of the game.

To deal with all the varied aspects of defensive play is beyond the scope of this book, and we must content ourselves with some fundamentals. One of the privileges enjoyed by the Defending Side is:

The Opening Lead
We saw on page 107 that the initial lead, by conferring an extra tempo on the Defenders, prevented the Declarer from establishing his long suit, and forced him to resort to a more speculative method of play to fulfil his Contract. You may then come to the conclusion that the initial lead is a great advantage.

That is true with the following proviso—*if you know what the right lead is.* But the wrong opening lead often gives away the Contract.

In this connection you have to know two things:

1. What suit to lead
2. What card of the suit to lead.

These again are dependent upon two other factors:

1. Whether partner has bid or not
2. Whether Contract is No Trumps or suit.

Before you go any further study the Table of Leads on pages 114 and 115.

Defence against No Trumps

Against a Contract of 3 NT the Defenders are intent on winning five Tricks. There are three possibilities:

1. That Declarer has nine cold Tricks and no lead makes any difference.

2. That Declarer has overbid and cannot make his Contract.

3. That Declarer can make his Contract if you fail to find the right defence.

To illustrate the third possibility let us examine the following:

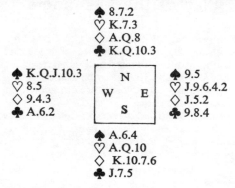

```
              ♠ 8.7.2
              ♡ K.7.3
              ◇ A.Q.8
              ♣ K.Q.10.3
♠ K.Q.J.10.3   ┌─────────────┐   ♠ 9.5
♡ 8.5          │    N        │   ♡ J.9.6.4.2
◇ 9.4.3        │  W     E    │   ◇ J.5.2
♣ A.6.2        │    S        │   ♣ 9.8.4
               └─────────────┘
              ♠ A.6.4
              ♡ A.Q.10
              ◇ K.10.7.6
              ♣ J.7.5
```

Bidding: North 1 ♣, South 3 NT

Examination shows us that South has one Spade, three Hearts and four Diamonds on top, with three easily establishable Clubs, a total of eleven Tricks. But you, West, have four establishable Spades and the ♣ A. You win the establishment race because the opening lead gives you that extra tempo. That is, of course, provided you lead the ♠ K! If you wasted your lead by opening any other suit you would give South his Contract. You know—or you should know—that if South requires even one Trick in Clubs to make his Contract he is doomed to defeat. So you follow the old maxim of leading longest and strongest against No Trumps. The table tells you to lead the King—the top of a sequence.

Let us alter West's Spade holding to K.J.9.5.3 and East's to Q.10. As before you lead a Spade, but this time you lead the fourth best (that is, the Five) because you have no sequence. Again the Contract is defeated. In both cases the hold-up of the ♠ A does not avail because the ♣ A is with West.

Let us now keep the original hands but change the bidding, and assume that North bids One (weak) No Trump which South raises to 3 NT. This time it is East's turn to make the opening lead. If he is a slave to 'longest and strongest' he leads the ♡ 4 and the Game is gone. Trying to establish the Heart suit is a lost cause. He will be squandering his partner's resources fruitlessly. His one hope is to employ his only asset—the initial lead—to promote his partner's Tricks. So he makes a short-suit lead of the ♠ 9, hoping to find his partner with strength in the suit. Thus East, too, defeats the Contract, not by following old saws but by an intelligent appraisal of the situation. It is the absence of any re-entry in East's hand that makes it a waste of time to play on the Heart suit. Look at it in this way. If West had bid Spades East would have opened the ♠ 9. East must assume that partner *has* a Spade suit which he was prevented from bidding. Of course, not all short-suit leads turn out as well as this, but sometimes one really strikes oil.

All the development plays open to the Declarer which were discussed in Chapter 18 are also open to the Defenders. But the Declarer, who sees the combined twenty-six cards, *knows* what Tricks can and cannot be developed. The Defenders can only *infer* what method will produce the required number of Tricks. You can see why defensive play is such a difficult department of the game. The hand just given illustrates development by force.

Similarly, the Defenders can make use of finesse, though the opportunities for repeating finesses (see page 97) is likely to be less than Declarer's, because of fewer entries. Suppose Dummy holds ♡ Q.5.3 and you, sitting over him, hold A.J.10. Your partner opens the ♡ 4. If you play the Ace you will set up Dummy's Queen for a Trick if partner has led from the King, and if he does not hold the King, you will set up both King and Queen as Tricks for the Declarer. So you rightly play the Ten. If partner has led from the King you prevent Declarer from making any Trick in the suit. If the Declarer has the King he can make it on the first Trick, but your A.J stands over the Queen. This is a correct finesse—a finesse against Dummy, but if Dummy had held ♡ 6.5.2 you would have been wrong to play the Ten. That is a *finesse against partner* and is to be avoided. You should have followed the 'rule' of Third Hand High and played your Ace.

You will notice that with A.J.10, when finessing against Dummy you played the Ten, not the Knave. This brings us to a most important principle of Third Hand play, that is the play of the leader's partner. If your highest cards are in sequence you must play the lowest. For example, if partner leads a small Heart and Dummy plays small, you with Q.J.10.3 play the Ten. Following suit with a card denies the one immediately below it. This procedure, as you see, is the opposite of that employed by the leader. Thus we have the rule: *Lead the highest card in a sequence, follow suit with the lowest in a sequence.*

The Defensive Duck

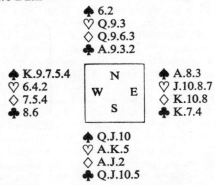

♠ 6.2
♡ Q.9.3
◇ Q.9.6.3
♣ A.9.3.2

♠ K.9.7.5.4   ♠ A.8.3
♡ 6.4.2   ♡ J.10.8.7
◇ 7.5.4   ◇ K.10.8
♣ 8.6   ♣ K.7.4

♠ Q.J.10
♡ A.K.5
◇ A.J.2
♣ Q.J.10.5

Against South's 3 NT West leads the Five of Spades. East wins and returns the Eight. If West takes this Trick the Contract is made. The Declarer plays the Knave and the Queen, but you know he is false-carding by your partner's return of the Eight. If he had held four he would have returned his lowest. If you duck this Trick, East when winning with the King of Clubs will still have a Spade to lead for you to defeat the Contract.

Defensive Unblocking

Third Hand must always be on the alert to unblock. Suppose a suit to be divided as follows:

9.5.4

Q.J.10.8.3 | W   E | K.6 (or A.6)

A.7.2 (or K.7.2)

West leads the Queen, and if in either case East fails to play the King (or Ace), the suit is blocked and a vital tempo is lost. These situations are obvious, but here is one that is a little more subtle:

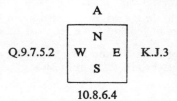

A

Q.9.7.5.2 | W   E | K.J.3

10.8.6.4

West leads the Five, and East must unblock by playing the Knave. This establishes a finesse position for West on the third round. If East does not unblock, West cannot overtake the Knave without setting up the Ten as a Trick. There are many variations of the defensive unblock.

The Rule of Eleven

Third Hand may make use of this legacy of Whist and Auction. When partner has led a fourth best you can learn a good deal about the location of the suit by this simple rule. You just subtract the number of 'pips' on the card led from eleven, and the result is the number of cards higher than the card led which are held by Dummy, the Declarer, and yourself. Take this simple case:

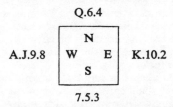

Q.6.4

A.J.9.8 | W   E | K.10.2

7.5.3

West's lead of the Eight shows three (11–8) cards higher than the card led in the other three hands. East can see all three—the

Queen in Dummy and the King and Ten in his own hand. He knows that Declarer has no card higher than the Eight.

Leading Partner's Suit

If partner has made a bid, you are no longer faced with a blind lead. You know something about your partner's hand. Though it may not always be right to lead partner's suit, you must have a very good reason for not doing so. If you do open his suit, what card do you lead? A number of people think that you must always lead the highest card, but this is only right

1. When you hold only two cards.
2. When you hold three cards not headed by an Honour.
3. When your holding includes two Honours in sequence.

When you hold three to an Honour lead the lowest, when you hold four or five lead the fourth best. Let us illustrate:

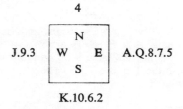

4

J.9.3   N W E A.Q.8.7.5   S

K.10.6.2

If West leads the Knave, South must take two Tricks in the suit, but the lead of the Three restricts him to one. A similar situation occurs if West has Q.9.3 and South has K.J.2. There are several variations.

Defence against a Suit Contract

Many of the conventions observed at No Trumps apply to suit play, but the basic approach is different. Against a suit Contract the small cards of a long suit will not normally be effective, so your aim is to establish winners quickly before the Declarer can draw trumps and establish a side suit for discards.

For a blind lead against a suit Contract nothing can be better than A.K.Q with no small cards. The lead of the King allows you to inspect the Dummy without jeopardizing any Trick. The lead from A.K.x, though high on the list, can give the Contract by allowing Declarer to set up Dummy's Queen for a vital discard.

Short Suit Lead

With the ruffing element present the leader may open a short suit, either a singleton or a doubleton, with a view to making a ruffing Trick or Tricks. The short suit lead is a two-edged weapon. When you choose the right moment it can defeat an otherwise impregnable Contract; when you choose the wrong moment it gives Declarer a normally unmakeable Contract by placing the cards for him.

Leading Trumps

The opening lead of a trump is based on the bidding, that is when Dummy's bidding discloses the ability to ruff. The most obvious case is when Declarer has bid two suits and Dummy is clearly short in the side suit. For example:

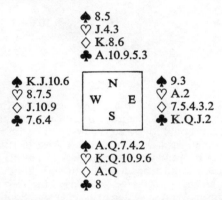

The bidding is South 1 ♠, North 1 NT, South 3 ♡, North 4 ♡.

Here the trump lead is obvious. East wins and returns a trump, and when West gets in with a Spade he leads a third round of trumps. This holds Declarer to nine Tricks. Without an opening trump lead South must make his Contract.

Leading Partner's Suit against Trump Contract

The same rules as for No Trumps mostly apply, but if you hold the Ace of partner's suit you must lead it if the suit is selected. When partner has bid, a singleton or doubleton in his suit is usually a desirable lead. Furthermore, the fact that partner has bid makes the lead of a singleton in another suit attractive, as there is more likelihood of getting him in to give you the ruff. If you hold A.x.x or K.x.x in trumps as well, then you really have chosen a good time to lead a singleton.

Signals

To conduct an intelligent defence the defenders must transmit *and receive* signals. Signals are cards played when not attempting to win a Trick. All signals are variations of the Echo (or Peter), which is the play of an unnecessarily high card, followed by a lower one on the next occasion. For example:

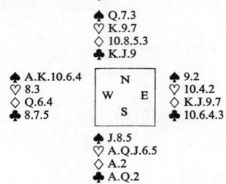

Against South's Contract of 4 ♡, West leads the King of Spades. Whether South makes his Contract or not depends upon what you, East, play. You should follow to the first Trick with the Nine—an unnecessarily high card. This encourages West to lead the Ace of Spades to Trick two, and you complete the Echo by playing the Two. West now leads a third Spade and you ruff. South must lose a Diamond so he goes down. Had you played the Two of Spades to Trick one, causing West to switch to another suit, South would have made ten Tricks.

Let us take another case, this time at No Trumps. Your partner leads ♠ Q from Q.J.9.4.3, Dummy has a singleton five, and you hold K.8.2. You should play the Eight, encouraging your partner to continue. If you play the Two, partner will switch, and the lost tempo may be enough for the Declarer.

You should make the same play if you hold 10.8.2, for partner has led from Q.J.9 and other cards, and it is essential for him to know that your Ten makes it safe for him to continue. You must notice that the Echo may not always be completed so quickly as in the first example. Indeed it may never be completed at all. So a player must be on the alert to interpret his partner's message from the unnecessarily high card. A Three followed by a Two is as much an Echo as a Ten followed by a Six, but for all that *when Echoing play as high a card as you can afford.*

The Echo can also be used when discarding. If Declarer leads a suit of which you are void, you may signal with a high card in another suit which you want partner to lead.

Special Echoes
(a) At No Trumps
There is a special form of high low signal employed against No Trumps Contracts, to inform partner how long it is necessary to hold up the top card of Dummy's long suit. For example:

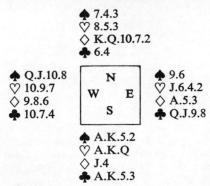

♠ 7.4.3
♡ 8.5.3
◇ K.Q.10.7.2
♣ 6.4

♠ Q.J.10.8   ♠ 9.6
♡ 10.9.7   ♡ J.6.4.2
◇ 9.8.6   ◇ A.5.3
♣ 10.7.4   ♣ Q.J.9.8

♠ A.K.5.2
♡ A.K.Q
◇ J.4
♣ A.K.5.3

Against 3 NT West leads the Queen of Spades. South wins and leads the Knave of Diamonds. West follows with the Six, and to the second Diamond lead plays the Eight. This failure to Echo denotes the holding of exactly three cards in the suit. This information tells East that it is safe to take the second round of Diamonds. If he ducked another Trick South would get home. If West had had only two Diamonds he would have Echoed, and East would have held up again to shut out the rest of the suit.

(b) In the Trump Suit
When a player Echoes in the trump suit it means that his original holding in the suit was three cards. It should also indicate that there is something that he can ruff. This Echo should be used when you are actually ruffing, to show partner that you can ruff a third time, if the opportunity occurs.

Echoing with an Honour
Holding a doubleton containing an Honour, it is in order to Echo if the Honour is Knave or Ten, but with the Queen it is incorrect.

The play of the Queen on partner's lead of the King shows either a singleton or the holding of the Knave as well. It is an unconditional demand on partner to play a small card to the next lead. This may be vital, as in the following example:

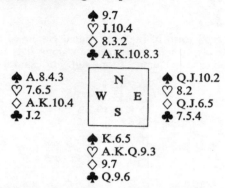

```
            ♠ 9.7
            ♡ J.10.4
            ◇ 8.3.2
            ♣ A.K.10.8.3

♠ A.8.4.3       N       ♠ Q.J.10.2
♡ 7.6.5    W        E   ♡ 8.2
◇ A.K.10.4              ◇ Q.J.6.5
♣ J.2           S       ♣ 7.5.4

            ♠ K.6.5
            ♡ A.K.Q.9.3
            ◇ 9.7
            ♣ Q.9.6
```

Against 4 ♡ West leads the King of Diamonds. You, East, play the Queen, demanding a small card from partner on the next lead. This enables you to get in with the Knave, and the lead of the Queen of Spades defeats South. No other play at Trick two can prevent South getting home.

In this chapter we have discussed but a small part of defensive play. From what you have read you should have learned some basic principles, but you will only become a good defensive player by concentration, and by learning from your own and other people's mistakes. Be comforted by the fact that even the expert has a great deal to learn about this department of the game.

Quiz on Chapter 21

1. Against a No Trumps Contract you decide to open Hearts. Which card do you lead from Q.J.9.7.2?

2. Against a No Trumps Contract you open Hearts, which partner bid. Which card do you lead from (a) Q.J.3? (b) Q.9.4?

3. Against a No Trumps Contract partner opens the King of Hearts. Which card do you play from J.8.3?

4. What is the reason for opening a trump?

Answers to Quizzes

Chapter 1

1. Spades and Hearts. 2. The player on the Dealer's left. 3. Spades, Hearts, Diamonds, Clubs. 4. The Four of Hearts. 5. (*a*) The first deal. (*b*) Choice of cards. (*c*) Choice of seats.

Chapter 2

1. When any bid, Double, or Re-double is followed by three consecutive calls of No Bid. 2. That member of the Declaring Side who *first* named the denomination of the Contract. 3. The deal is abandoned and the next player in rotation deals with the other pack. 4. The first six Tricks won by the Declarer. 5. West.

Chapter 3

1. Below the line by the Declaring Side. 2. 500. 3. 130 below the line and 60 above. 4. (*a*) 50. (*b*) 50. 5. Penalty Points and Honour Points.

Chapter 4

1. A method of hand valuation: Ace = 4, King = 3, Queen = 2, Knave = 1. 2. To force opponents to accept Penalty Points instead of Trick Points. 3. 20. 4. Place = Denomination, Height = Number of Tricks contracted for. 5. First- and second-round winners.

Chapter 5

2. NT on 1. 3. NT on 3. 1 NT on 5. Hand 2 has a worthless doubleton. Hand 4 has the wrong pattern.

Chapter 6

1. No Bid. 2. 6 NT. 3. 4 NT. 4. 4 NT. 5. 3 NT.

Chapter 7

1. (*a*) A biddable suit. (*b*) Two Defensive Tricks and 12 Points. (*c*) A guaranteed rebid if partner makes a call other than No Trumps or a raise of your suit. 2. Bid higher-ranking suit first.

2. Bid higher-ranking suit first.
    Yes, with Spades and Clubs and a near minimum.

3. 1. 1 Diamond. 2. 1 Spade. 3. 1 Club.

Chapter 8

1. 3 ♡. 2. 2 NT. 3. No Bid. 4. 2 ♣. 5. 1 ♠.

Chapter 9

1. 3 NT. 2. 3 NT. 3. 3 ♠. 4. 4 ♡. 5. 2 ♣.

Chapter 10

1. 2 ♡. 2. 2 NT. 3. 3 ♠. 4. 2 ◇. 5. 3 NT.

Chapter 11

1. No Bid. 2. 3 ◇. 3. 2 ◇. 4. 3 NT. 5. 4 ♠.

Chapter 12

On 2. Pass on 1. 1 ♠ on 3.
4. You cannot play in 3 NT when you want to. 5. 5 ♡.

Chapter 13

1. 2 ♣. 2. 2 ♠. 3. 1 ♠. 4. 3 ♠. 5. 4 ♠.

Chapter 14

1. 5 ♡. 2. 4 NT—to find out if partner has two Aces.
3. 3 ◇—to mark the Club singleton when you later raise Spades.

Chapter 15

1. 3 ♡. 2. Double. 3. No Bid. 4. Double. 5. 4 ◇.

Chapter 16

1. 2 NT. 2. 2 NT. 3. No Bid. 4. Double. 5. 2 ♠.

Chapter 17

No Quiz—Re-read Doubles of Competitive Bids at the Lower Levels.

Chapter 18

1. Honour Cards, Long Cards, Ruffs.
2. An attempt to exploit positional advantage, by winning a Trick with a card not the highest in the suit.
3. Lead Ace and then small to the Queen.
4. Duck the first round. 5. Lead the Two and finesse the Nine.

Chapter 19

1. Count established winners, count establishable winners, count opponents' winners.

2. A counter-duck, to force opponents to take their Tricks when it is disadvantageous to do so.

3. (*a*) No. (*b*) No. (*c*) No.

Chapter 20

1. *Any three of:* To discard losers. To ruff losers. To avoid forcing the long hand. To preserve entry.

2. Cash side suit winners. 3. A Heart and finesse the Queen.

Chapter 21

1. Queen. 2. (*a*) Queen. (*b*) Four. 3. Eight. 4. To cut down Dummy's ruffing power.